Every Day with Jesus

NOV/DEC 2020

More Than Conquerors

'If God is for us, who can be against us?' Romans 8:31

Selwyn Hughes
Revised and updated by Mick Brooks

© CWR 2020. Dated text previously published as *The Great Divide* (Nov/Dec 2007) by CWR. This edition revised and updated for 2020 by Mick Brooks.

CWR, Waverley Abbey House, Waverley Lane, Farnham, Surrey GU9 8EP, UK **Tel: 01252 784700**
Email: mail@cwr.org.uk Registered Charity No. 294387. Registered Limited Company No. 1990308.

Cover image: Unsplash/Christopher Campbell
Quiet Time image: Gerd Altmann
Printed in England by Linney

MIX
Paper from
responsible sources
FSC® C015900
www.fsc.org

Every Day with Jesus is available in large print from CWR. It is also available on **audio and DAISY** in the UK and Eire for the sole use of those with a visual impairment worse than N12, or who are registered blind. For details please contact **Torch Trust for the Blind**, Tel: 01858 438260. Torch House, Torch Way, Northampton Road, Market Harborough LE16 9HL.

A word of introduction...

Many things have been said about the Bible, but one thing you can't say is that it sugar-coats or 'airbrushes' the lives of those whose stories it recounts. It doesn't pull any punches – it's all there in black and white. It's a real book, with real-life stories, a no-holds-barred exposé that any journalist would have been glad to put their name to. In our final issue of the year, we'll be unpacking some remarkable verses from Paul's letter to the Romans that help us to understand what it means to live as 'more than a conqueror' and, just as importantly, what it doesn't mean. Despite what we might have liked, God has never promised that if we follow Him, like some divine insurance policy, we will dance through life unscathed. It was, after all, Jesus Himself who said, 'In this world you will have trouble' (John 16:33). See, it isn't sugar-coated!

In times of struggle and uncertainty, words are helpful, but ultimately it is presence and connection with others that makes the biggest difference. Rarely do we remember what people say, but we never forget how they made us feel. Later this issue, we'll reflect specifically on Christmas – the remarkable event that forever changed the world, when God stepped out of eternity to live among us. Because of His astonishing arrival in Bethlehem, we can know God as Immanuel, God with us. As we surrender our lives into His hands, the slate is wiped clean and we are assured of God's promised presence, blessed to live as 'more than conquerors'.

God bless,

Mick

Mick Brooks, Consulting Editor

New wineskins

FOR READING & MEDITATION – MATTHEW 9:9–17
'people... pour new wine into new wineskins' (v17)

The theme for the closing weeks of this year is taken from Paul's superlative statement in Romans 8:37: 'we are more than conquerors through him who loved us'. What's fascinating about the New Testament is the way in which language had to bear a whole new weight of meaning with Jesus' coming into the world. Up until that time, human language had proved enough to communicate the truths that men and women needed to understand. But when Jesus came, it needed to express insights that were new and very profound. And that is perhaps no more clearly demonstrated than when Paul boldly declared, 'We are more than conquerors through him who loved us' (Rom. 8:37). It would have been extraordinary enough if Paul had said, 'We are conquerors through Him who loved us', but he put in the added emphasis – 'more than conquerors'. Is this mere overstatement, exaggeration? No – it's a plain statement of fact.

FURTHER STUDY

Matt. 12:1–14;
1 John 5:4–5

1. How did the Pharisees respond to Jesus' new teaching?

2. What conquers the world?

In Jesus, the Godhead had broken through into human life; and language, which was called upon to express the realities of that awesome truth, sometimes proved unequal to the task. The early Christians had to use one superlative after another in order to convey this amazing truth. The new wine of God's wonderful grace-filled plan had not only to be put into the new wineskins of ministry and organisation, but also into the new wineskins of a new vocabulary.

Here was a brand-new set of facts. To be a conqueror is one thing; to be more than a conqueror is another. That word 'more' is a window that allows us to see the inexhaustible nature of our resources and the unlimited development that lies before us. In Jesus we do much more than survive. We can thrive.

Father, I see that this is one 'more' that really counts. As I look through this 'window' at the resources available to me in Jesus, help me to take hold of those resources and live as You originally planned. In Christ's name I pray. Amen.

Old word, new content

FOR READING & MEDITATION – JOHN 15:9–25

'love each other as I have loved you.' (v12)

Yesterday we saw that with Jesus' coming into the world, language had to be stretched to convey the implications of the salvation He enabled. The early Christians had to adapt old words or use superlatives to express their meaning. Take, for example, the development of the word 'love'.

There were different words for 'love' in the Greek language during the time of Jesus, including *eros* and *agape*. Greek writers, especially Plato, used the word *eros* to express the idea of love for the creator or His creatures, whereas Christians opted for the word *agape*. And even the meaning Christians put into *agape* did not reflect its Greek source. They adopted the word and gave it a content that it never had before. *Agape*, when filled with Christian meaning, encapsulates the most revolutionary idea ever presented to the human mind. Anders Nygren, an authority on the use of Greek words, said: 'In ancient times two men commented about God: Plato – "God is *eros*"; John – "God is *agape*". Just the difference of two words but behind them the difference of two worlds.'

FURTHER STUDY

Ruth 1:1–18;
Eph. 5:1–2;
1 Cor. 13

1. Contrast the love of Ruth and Orpah for Naomi.

2. How are we to love?

Over time *eros* has come to be associated with sexual love, and *agape* with the love of the God. This is because Christian content has been put into *agape*; a word that in its original usage was distinctly human has become one of the best vehicles for expressing the love that reaches down to us from heaven. When we think of *eros* we think of human passion; when we think of *agape* we think of God's self-giving love shown to us in His incarnate Son. The new content put into the *agape* love of God in Christ is the dividing line in humanity – all life and all systems line themselves up on one side or the other.

Father, I see that *eros* has a place, but that the highest form of love is *agape*. Help me to see and know You in the light of Your *agape* love. May Your *agape* create *agape* in me. Amen.

God help grammar

FOR READING & MEDITATION – EPHESIANS 3:1–21

*'Now to him who is able to do immeasurably more than all we ask
or imagine' (v20)*

Today we continue thinking about how language had to bear a whole new weight of meaning with the coming of Jesus into the world. Language which had once been adequate to express human concepts was now called upon to express divine–human relationships.

Today's text shows how language was stretched to convey the thought that God is able to do far more than we could ever ask or imagine. Although we use the NIV translation for our meditations, we sometimes get a fuller picture of what the passage is saying by looking at other translations alongside it. Note the translation in the New King James Version: 'Now to Him who is able to do exceedingly abundantly above all that we ask or think'. 'Exceedingly abundantly' – this phrase comes much closer to the thought in the original Greek. You get the feeling that Paul, as he writes, is leaping over all boundaries, widening all horizons and blowing away all restrictions in an effort to let us see how good and great God is. Words are being stretched and superlatives being used because the truth of what he is saying is far too big to cram into just one word.

FURTHER STUDY

1 Cor. 2:6–16;
Eph. 1:15–23

1. How can we understand the deep things of God?

2. To what does Paul compare God's power?

One theologian who has studied the language of the early disciples says that there are times when their enthusiasm resulted in the disorganisation of their grammar. As a writer I've tried to pay considerable attention to grammar, but there are times when I've felt great sympathy with D.L. Moody. Reprimanded by a grammar pedant over a sentence structure he had made, he replied: 'Madam, when I see souls going to hell and grammar gets in the way – then God help grammar.' Sometimes grammatical rules can't bear the pressure of this new, outstanding, vibrant life.

Father, sometimes the reality of what You have done for me in Jesus becomes so overwhelming that words become inadequate. This new wine needs new wineskins. Hallelujah! Amen.

'More than'

FOR READING & MEDITATION – ROMANS 8:18–39

'No, in all these things we are more than conquerors through him who loved us.' (v37)

First, the word 'more' in today's text stands out in a powerful and particular way. As we said three days ago, it is the 'more' that counts. It is the 'plus' which is characteristic of the Christian faith, and that sets it apart from every other religion. The 'more' invites people to outstrip the ordinary level of the everyday, in purpose, in peace and rest, and in emotional and mental wellbeing. In the struggle of life, it is the extra resilience of endurance, that extra inner strength that Christians have at their disposal, which keeps them from falling apart when everything is breaking up all around them.

FURTHER STUDY

2 Cor. 1:3–11;
Phil. 4:10–13

1. How did Paul conquer his situation?

2. Why can we be more than a conqueror?

The very first testimony I gave in public contained these words: 'I have tried by sheer willpower to break bad habits in my life, but they have beaten me every time. Since I gave my life to Jesus, I have been conscious of a new-found strength and resilience at work within me that carries me past the temptations that I once fell prey to.' After many decades of living the Christian life, I was able to testify that that power never leaves a true child of God but continues to work in their lives and personality (see Rom. 8:11).

But what does it mean to be 'more than a conqueror'? There is the story of a little boy in Sunday school who, when asked that question, replied: 'To be a conqueror means to win by fighting; to be more than a conqueror means to win without fighting.' Well, it is not a perfect explanation because the Christian life is not one of passivity, but it is a good start. We are more than conquerors because we are held by the one at whose name every knee will one day bow.

Father, how reassuring it is to know that in the race of life You provide the strength and resilience to enable me to be more than a conqueror. I am so thankful. Amen.

CWR Ministry Events

Please pray for the team

With the extraordinary circumstances we have needed to adapt to this year, we remain committed to delivering biblically based courses and events that connect you to God, His Word and each other. Whether in person at Waverley Abbey House, or via online platforms enabling you to engage with our training from the comfort and safety of your own home, we trust you will join us and continue to be taught, inspired and encouraged by our programme of events.

For the latest information, please visit our website: **cwr.org.uk/courses** and follow us on Facebook where we will keep you up to date with dates and booking information.

We are still offering a full College programme, and value your ongoing prayers for all our staff and students at Waverley Abbey College as they continue their studies in Counselling and Spiritual Formation.

For further information and a full list of CWR's courses, seminars and events, call **(+44) 01252 784719** or visit **cwr.org.uk/courses**

You can also download our free Prayer Track, which includes weekly prayer points, from **cwr.org.uk/prayertrack**

Monochrome living

FOR READING & MEDITATION – REVELATION 1:1–8

'to him be glory and power for ever and ever!' (v6)

Everyone who follows Jesus needs to, at least occasionally, reflect on this incisive and challenging question: Does my life reflect the truth that in Jesus I am 'more than a conqueror' (Rom. 8:37)? Do I start each day sure and confident that nothing can happen that day which Jesus and I cannot handle together? This is a tough challenge, but it's important to ask.

It is because the Word became flesh that we have the resources not only to meet problems head on, but to stand in the middle of them. I am not talking about triumphalism now, just simple reality. During a conference in Asia at which I was invited to speak, I heard another speaker comment: 'The chief characteristic of modern-day Christianity is non-expectancy.' I remember thinking: I hope what he says isn't true, because if it is then the situation is extremely serious. When we expect nothing to happen, nothing will. How sad it is to see in some parts of the world the awful power that fatalism can have in limiting otherwise talented and capable people, causing them to throw up their hands in helpless resignation. But what is worse is to see Christians settle down in a spirit of non-expectancy and live out their lives in spiritual and emotional paralysis.

FURTHER STUDY

Acts 3:1–19

1. What did the crippled man expect to receive?

2. What did Peter and John expect him to receive?

Dr Worcester, an American doctor and a Christian, had many years' experience of working in clinics which, though not exclusively Christian, were geared to the needs of believers. He once said: 'Most Christians do not expect their religion to do them any great or immediate good. They do not even see themselves as conquerors, let alone more than conquerors.' That seems a very monochrome way to go through life.

Father God, strengthen me when my energy is low. Help me to expect and receive You and Your presence in all I do and am. Please help me live life to the full. In Jesus' name. Amen.

Defeat needn't be normal

FOR READING & MEDITATION – ROMANS 15:1–13

'that you may overflow with hope by the power of the Holy Spirit.' (v13)

Although it is unrealistic to imagine we will spend our entire Christian life on the mountain tops and never enter into the valley of doubt or disillusionment, it is not unrealistic to discover that by far the largest experience of our faith life is characterised by peace and contentment. Yesterday we quoted a doctor who commented, 'Most Christians do not expect their religion to do them any great or immediate good.' The doctor went on to explain that when he told his patients that their condition of moral and spiritual defeat need not be permanent but that they could live a more joyful life, they would look at him in disbelief. They had accepted defeat as being normal.

Another doctor tells the story of a little girl suffering from a condition which made it difficult for her to stand straight. After treating her for a while, he enabled her to stand quite straight and said, 'Now walk to your mother.' She walked perfectly straight for the first time in years and then, bursting into tears, threw herself into her mother's arms and cried, 'Mummy, I'm all crooked.'

Can it be that there are people in today's Church who think being spiritually straight and upstanding is something strange and unnatural? It would seem that this is so. Perhaps some Christians do not expect anything beyond repeated forgiveness for constantly repeated thoughts and behaviours. They certainly do not expect to be able to live differently. This attitude of non-expectancy is something we need to understand and resolve. Those who follow Jesus as their deliverer and Saviour do not need to allow themselves to expect that defeat is normal.

FURTHER STUDY

Num. 13:26–14:4;
Josh. 14:6–12

1. What was Caleb's attitude to difficulties?

2. What was the Israelites' attitude?

Dear Father, You are revealing our need and Your hope. Help us to live the way You want us to live and enjoy Your peace and hope-filled life. Whatever happens, save us from expecting defeat to be normal. In Christ's name we pray. Amen.

Strength and resilience

FOR READING & MEDITATION – ROMANS 8:1–8

'the law of the Spirit who gives life has set you free from the law of sin and death.' (v2)

We said yesterday that some Christians do not expect anything beyond repeated forgiveness for constantly repeated thoughts and behaviours. Does this mean we can live as we please because there is forgiveness if we ask? Is this all we can expect for our lives, an endless cycle of mistakes and failures? Is forgiveness for constantly repeated thoughts and behaviours the best we can expect? If it is, then the Christian gospel offers freedom, but with no energy, strength and resilience to live the way that God originally intended.

FURTHER STUDY

Rom. 6:1–14; 7:21–25

1. What parts do we and God play in overcoming sin?

2. Why is God's grace not limited to forgiveness?

A number of world religions believe they will have to pay for their sins – the law of karma, which defines a person's future, is dependent on what they have done in their past. For them there is no forgiveness. An American missionary who renounced his Christian beliefs and became a Hindu said that he wanted his children brought up under karma rather than redemption, because the message of constantly repeated forgiveness for constantly repeated sins would weaken their characters. 'It would make them flabby,' he said.

The gospel does offer forgiveness for sin, but along with it, and as a part of it, we are offered the strength and grace to overcome sin. Forgiveness and inner strength are binding aspects of the grace of God. If we receive forgiveness without the inner resilience and resolve then we will be faced with continual struggle and tension. We do not need to stay in the dark places of life – we can receive God's forgiveness, and this releases an inner resilience that enables us to climb (albeit one step at a time) to become all that He longs for us to become.

Father, what a joy it is to know that in You I find not only forgiveness for all the sins of the past, but strength to overcome sin in the future and to live as You originally designed. For this I am eternally grateful. Amen.

No immunity!

FOR READING & MEDITATION – JAMES 1:1–18

'God cannot be tempted by evil, nor does he tempt anyone' (v13)

Before we go on to look at what it means in practice to be 'more than conquerors' (Rom. 8:37), let's think about what Paul did *not* mean when he made this statement.

First, it does *not* mean that we will be immune to temptation. Second, today's reading makes it absolutely plain that temptation does not come from God. The passage continues: 'but each person is tempted when they are dragged away by their own evil desire and enticed. Then, after desire has conceived, it gives birth to sin' (vv14–15). Notice we are not dragged away by temptation but by our 'own evil desire'. In other words, it is not the temptation that produces sin. *The Message* paraphrase reads: 'The temptation to give in to evil comes from us and only us'. Temptation is not sin; it is only when we 'go with it' and let it grow and take root that it becomes sin. No one can stop the suggestion of malicious, jealous or lustful thoughts entering our minds, but we can stop nurturing them and brooding over them. Dismissed at once, they leave no mark; held and entertained by the mind, they can discolour everything. It's an old saying that you can't stop the crows flying over your head but you can stop them making a nest in your hair.

FURTHER STUDY

1 Cor. 10:1–13;
1 Tim. 6:9–12

1. How can we escape temptation?

2. What should we pursue?

There is, however, one positive aspect to the ugly issue of temptation. Goethe said, 'Difficulties prove men.' When Jesus went into the desert to be tempted by the devil 'full of the Holy Spirit' (Luke 4:1), and came out 'in the power of the Spirit' (Luke 4:14), fullness turned to power under the pressure of temptation. Being 'more than a conqueror', then, does not mean being immune from temptation, but coming through with an inner strength and resolve.

Lord Jesus, You left the desert of temptation stronger than when You went into it. Please help me to follow Your example. Walk with me into my struggles and enable me to make temptation contribute to my spiritual growth, I pray. Amen.

Purity is not maturity

FOR READING & MEDITATION – 1 SAMUEL 16:1–13

'People look at the outward appearance, but the LORD looks at the heart.' (v7)

Being 'more than a conqueror', as we began to see yesterday, does not mean we will not be tempted. Nor does it guarantee us freedom from making mistakes. It's important to remind ourselves that, whatever our age, our characters are still being refined and developed, and that at present we are still grappling with issues that are too great for us to comprehend fully. This does not mean we lower the standards, but it does mean that sometimes, with the best will in the world, we will make mistakes. 'The man who never made a mistake,' says an old proverb, 'never made anything.' Our actions are the result of our intentions and our knowledge. Though our intentions may be very good, because our knowledge is limited, the action may result in a mistake – a mistake, but not necessarily a sin. Sin results from a wrong intention. Many things we do may hurt others, and for these we need to apologise, but they are not necessarily intentional. The action may have carried a sense of incompleteness and frustration, but not of guilt.

FURTHER STUDY

Matt. 15:1–20

1. Why were the Pharisees offended?

2. What did Jesus explain?

In addition to the many mistakes we may make in our lives there will also be the signs of our immaturity. Immaturity is not inconsistent with being 'more than a conqueror'. We might confuse the two, but purity is not maturity. When my children were very young, one of them wrote me a letter while I was overseas. It was covered with many smudges and contained many mistakes. Was it mature? No. Was it pure? Yes. I saw through the immaturity to the intention, and that made all the difference. It is the same with God. He doesn't want His children to stay immature, of course – what parent does – but He sees the intentions of the heart.

Father, this gospel of ours is called 'the way'. Our feet are on the way, but we have not arrived at our destination. Help me to walk on that way, and at the right pace – not too slowly and not too fast. In Jesus' name. Amen.

Crying for the Shepherd

FOR READING & MEDITATION – ISAIAH 55:1–13

*'turn to the LORD, and he will have mercy... and to our God,
for he will freely pardon.' (v7)*

Being 'more than a conqueror' does not guarantee freedom from making mistakes; neither does it mean that we will never again have a malicious thought or behave badly.

When I said this in a meeting, a man took me to task for making it easy for people to do as they please and, in his view, opening the door to do what you like. He argued: 'If you focus people's attention on the truth that when they sin they can find instant forgiveness, it will make them weak Christians. They will go for the soft option whenever they are under pressure.' While I understood what he was saying, and although this provision is not our primary focus, nevertheless it is there in Scripture (1 John 1:9 – 'If we confess our sins'), and so he turned away without further comment. Though we may be totally committed to living for God, it's a real blessing and a gift from God that there is provision for us when we sin. Our focus is not on the provision, but that we can receive forgiveness from God whenever it is necessary.

When we do fall short in our relationship with Jesus and with others, what then? We ask God's forgiveness for it, and then set about righting any wrongs that may be necessary. We may have lost a skirmish, but that does not mean we have lost the battle. Indeed, we may even lose a battle, but we can still win the war. One of the differences between a sheep and a pig is that when a sheep falls into a mud pit, it bleats and bleats until it gets out. When a pig falls into a mud pit, it loves it and would wallow in it for ever. A true and growing Christian is someone who begins the day by strengthening themselves in the resilience that God offers for the day ahead.

FURTHER STUDY

Luke 15:3–7;
1 John 1:5–10

1. How does Jesus feel about His sheep who have strayed?

2. Why may we be deceived?

Father, help me in my thinking about these two issues – the strength available and the provision of forgiveness. Every day, help me to think not so much that it is possible to sin, but that it is possible not to sin. In Jesus' name. Amen.

A spiritual diarchy

FOR READING & MEDITATION – 1 JOHN 5:1–5

'everyone born of God overcomes the world.' (v4)

Over the past few days we have seen what being 'more than a conqueror' does not mean; now we think about what it does mean. It means, quite simply, allowing Jesus into every part of our life and in all our relationships, and living well, as God intended.

Many Christians allow Jesus to influence some areas of their lives, while other areas are withheld. Over these reserved areas we make the rules, we make the decisions. This introduces the principle of duality into life – frequently this causes inner division and tension. In India, between 1921 and 1937, the British devised a system of government where power was shared between the British and the Indians. That kind of government is called a 'diarchy'. Inevitably, the system collapsed, just as any attempt to have a spiritual diarchy within the personality eventually fails. Many Christians set up a spiritual diarchy, and then wonder why their spiritual life is such a struggle and dissatisfying. It's simply not possible to be at a peace and rest when there is an inner division and tension. If there's no unity within, sadly, collapse will be inevitable.

FURTHER STUDY

Luke 18:18–25;
James 1:5–8

1. What diarchy did the ruler have?

2. What is the result of double-mindedness?

I have met many Christians who have struggled, saying 'I am a Christian, but I am far from experiencing what the Bible describes as living "abundantly". Why?' After talking and praying together it often led to one place – a spiritual diarchy. They have enough of the love of Jesus in their lives to make them miserable. By that I mean they have received the love of God into their lives, but only so far – far enough to give them a taste of what life is all about but not far enough to walk into all that God has promised.

Lord Jesus, forgive us when we make You a half-King, leaving other half-gods in our hearts. We realise that this place of tension can only collapse. Forgive us and help us to see You in all Your greatness. For Your dear name's sake. Amen.

Spiritual Formation at
Waverley Abbey College

'Spiritual Formation has broadened my concept of my heavenly Father, and strengthened my faith by challenging what I believe God is doing in every part of life. God is good, and this course helps us see our spiritual lives more clearly.' – Steve (student)

At Waverley Abbey College, our successful Spiritual Formation programme will soon be entering its third year. From the beginning, we have supported students to reach their full potential, and this year will be no different.

While engaging in knowledge and conceptual frameworks drawn from theology, psychology, social sciences, historical studies, counselling, leadership studies and psychotherapy, students also benefit from time spent in prayer and devotion.

There are many options to learn within the Spiritual Formation programme, with teaching from practitioners and academics in their field of expertise. Options include university validated Higher Education options, as well as single module choices in:

· Mentoring and Coaching
· Chaplaincy
· Pastoral Care
·Spiritual Direction

These are extraordinary times, bringing about an altered pace of life with challenges for many. The need for spiritual guidance continues, and the modules that we teach equip people with the skills and tools to help others grow and develop in their Christian faith.

To find out more, please visit
waverleyabbeycollege.ac.uk/online-open-day

Duality brings disaster

FOR READING & MEDITATION – REVELATION 3:14–22

'you are neither cold nor hot. I wish you were either one or the other!' (v15)

Yesterday we made the comment that some people have 'enough of the love of Jesus in their lives to make them miserable'. To avoid being misunderstood, let me try to clarify more fully what I mean.

When we restrict Jesus' access to the very core of our personalities and do not follow His guidance and instructions in all areas of our lives, this creates a conflict and inner turmoil between opposing ideas, and we live in a state of tension. Let there be no doubt about it – God's ideas are often in conflict with our ideas. So deeply embedded in our nature is self-centredness that we frequently think we are doing things for God's glory when, in reality, we are doing them to boost our self-esteem and status. This tension does not always become apparent to the conscious mind, but it is certainly apparent to the unconscious mind.

One writer says, rather boldly: 'Either you must dismiss Christ entirely from your life and forget Him, and take over the entire control in your own hands, in which case you will be unified under the control of self. Or you must make a complete surrender of every withheld area into the control of Christ, in which case the life will be Christ-controlled, and therefore unified.' Personally, I find myself reacting very strongly against the option of dismissing Christ entirely from one's life. Rather, I encouraged people to take the second option – to make a complete surrender of every area being withheld into His care. The big issue is that there can be no real peace and happiness in the heart of someone who has areas of their life into which Jesus is not invited. Duality does not exist in the soul without disaster.

FURTHER STUDY

1 Kings 11:1–11;
James 4:8–10

1. Why was Solomon unwise?

2. What are the double-minded to do?

Father, I realise that to live well, You ask me to trust You entirely and not just in part. Please help me bring everything under Your sway and Your care because the rightness of doing so is clear. Amen.

A 'DIY' lifestyle

FOR READING & MEDITATION – ROMANS 7:7–25

'What a wretched man I am! Who will rescue me from this body that is subject to death?' (v24)

Today we ask: why is it that we resist and struggle to allow and invite Jesus into every area of our lives? Largely, it is because we like things to be under our control.

The sin which Adam and Eve committed in the Garden of Eden was a declaration of independence. One of the consequences of their action was to set off a chain reaction down throughout humankind; the original 'do it yourself' attitude. When Jesus stands before us asking us to follow Him, the feelings that arise within are those of vulnerability and distrust. This goes against the grain of our personalities because we know it means living in dependence on God instead of on our self-sufficiency, so we try to compromise.

We say to Jesus, albeit unconsciously: 'I will let You have some areas of my life – just enough to enable me to still have some feeling of independence. But don't ask me to experience that vulnerable feeling of complete and total dependence.' That, however, is what God does ask of those who say they want to be committed to Him. He wants us to be willing to trust Him enough to experience that feeling of vulnerability and give ourselves completely to Him. A life of true peace involves total dependence on Jesus, and the willingness to cease living as a self-centred person and to live instead as a Christ-centred one.

FURTHER STUDY

Luke 9:57–62;
14:25–35

1. What did Jesus explain about being His disciple?

2. What are we to carry and what to lay down?

Who doesn't struggle with this issue? Who doesn't prefer to hold on to the visible securities of life, even when they are falling apart? The question is, can we trust our lives to God? Or do we want to continue in our way, committed to a DIY lifestyle? The invitation stands today as Jesus stands at the door of our hearts.

Lord God, I want to trust You more than the things I can touch and see. Help me from this day to live in dependence on You and know You as El Shaddai – The One who is Enough. In Jesus' name. Amen.

'In all these things'

FOR READING & MEDITATION – ISAIAH 41:1–16

*'do not fear, for I am with you; do not be dismayed,
for I am your God.' (v10)*

To help us fully understand and realise its impact on our daily lives, it's important that we do not overlook how the verse we are focusing on for our mediations begins with the words: '*in all these things* we are more than conquerors through him who loved us' (Rom. 8:37, emphasis added). The words 'in all these things' bring an intense realism to what might otherwise be seen as mere optimism. I say 'realism', for in the Christian faith there is no avoidance of the difficulties which confront those who are living a God-dependent life.

FURTHER STUDY

Matt. 7:24–27;
2 Cor. 4:7–18

1. Why is it foolish to ignore Christ's teachings?

2. What was Paul's testimony?

In this verse, Paul is not taking an ostrich-like attitude – the attitude of someone who puts their head in the sand and says, 'There are no problems.' Instead, he demonstrates an open-eyed frankness and admits, 'Yes, I see there are many difficulties – distress, persecution, hunger, nakedness, danger of the sword, death, life, things present and things to come – but nevertheless, in all these things, we are more than conquerors.' This approach is completely honest, and yet still he asserts the central truth of hope and redemption.

Those who handle life by pretending there are no problems are simply building their houses on sand (see Matt. 7:26). Any attempt to establish life on the sands of denial rather than on the rock of reality is inviting failure. Denial is an attempt to dethrone God. It suggests that God is not quite big enough to handle whatever we have to face. The work of keeping reality at bay, however, also requires a great deal of personal energy. That is why people who live in denial are often 'weary' with the world. They work so hard at keeping God and reality apart that they have little or no energy left for life.

Lord God, forgive me if denial is something I use to survive. Give me such a vision of Yourself that I will be able to face whatever comes, knowing that it cannot overthrow You and that You are with me. Thank You, my Father. Amen.

The way of realism

'My prayer is not that you take them out of the world but that you protect them from the evil one.' (v15)

Today we continue looking at the truth of 'in all these things we are more than conquerors through him who loved us' (Rom. 8:37). The things Paul mentions in Romans 8:35–39 are not pleasant or agreeable, but deeply upsetting: 'trouble, hardship, persecution, famine, nakedness, danger, sword'. A worse combination is scarcely imaginable. And yet Paul says that 'in all these things' – not in some of them – we are overcomers. We are not resilient in some things and defeated in others, but in every one of them we are more than conquerors. That means, as we have already seen, that we are conquerors with a margin, a plus, ready for another encounter, with our resources intact.

FURTHER STUDY

2 Cor. 11:23–33; 12:7–10

1. What was Paul's experience?

2. How did he overcome weakness?

I would like to say some more about that little word 'in'. What is its relationship with 'things'? Does spirituality include the world of the physical and the material? World religions and popular philosophies all have a view, suggesting many different approaches. Some say we must be indifferent to all things; others say we are beyond all things or that we should be apart from all things, or even through all things. The teaching given in some cults and sects is to deny all things. Every one of these approaches and ideologies aims for life that is indifferent to things. Only Jesus offers us the inner strength to be more than conquerors *in* all things.

This highlights that Jesus is the way of realism, not idealism. That word 'in' conveys relationship to, and yet not identification with, all things. It signifies realistic contact, yet inward resilience to stand. Our peace and place of rest is not in being indifferent to things – apart from things – but is gained 'in all… things'.

Thank You, Lord Jesus, that You, the Word who became flesh, walked and lived in the middle of all things. I need not run away from anything, for through Your strength and grace I can be a conqueror in everything. Amen.

Not blinkered or blind

FOR READING & MEDITATION – 2 CORINTHIANS 6:1–13

'dying, and yet we live on; beaten, and yet not killed' (v9)

Yesterday we said that in the Christian life, hope and resilience are not apart from, but in all things. Living the Jesus way does not bear things in the way of stoicism; nor make you indifferent to things; nor deny the reality of things; nor buckle under things; nor expect to escape from things by trying to earn God's favour through a performance-based religion; nor become immersed in things as in materialism. Rather, it offers us the possibility of using everything that comes – good, bad, or indifferent, as we say – and making something out of it.

FURTHER STUDY

Acts 16:16–34

1. How did Paul and Silas respond to persecution?

2. What was the result?

We are not blinkered by things or blinded by them. In walking with Jesus there is no escapist mentality, no playing tricks on the universe, no side-stepping of any issues. Our spirituality can be shown to be in relationship to things. Those who try to be spiritual by ignoring the real issues of life possibly end up with a pseudo-spirituality. They are so heavenly minded that they are no earthly good.

Paul, in Romans 8:38–39, identifies ten things that cannot separate us from the love of God – the same love that sent Jesus to earth. When he lists these ten things, he is not intending to limit the Christian hope to just these possibilities. In reality he is saying, 'Nothing, nothing, can break you when you are hidden in Christ.' Someone has called these 'the ten horses of evil' that try to chase and ride us down and trample us under their feet. We learn, however, that we need not let these 'horses of evil' ride us down. Instead, we can grasp their bridles, swing into their saddles, and ride them to our own destination. When we learn how to do that we are learning how to live in Jesus.

Lord Jesus, Thank You for coming and living Your life among us. Thank You that I can go into today with confidence that life won't trample over me or overwhelm me because You are with me. Amen.

'Room to grow up in'

FOR READING & MEDITATION – 1 CORINTHIANS 15:12–28

'The last enemy to be destroyed is death.' (v26)

Let's look more closely at 'the ten horses of evil' (Rom. 8:38–39) we referred to yesterday. Take the first: 'death'. Paul puts the most unknown first, as death is undoubtedly one of humanity's greatest fears.

Some people refuse to discuss the subject of death because it produces feelings in them they would rather not face. A lawyer once told me that one reason why so many avoid making a will is because they don't want to accept the reality of their own mortality. A gracious elderly Christian lady, with whom I lodged for a while when I was a young minister, said, 'I look forward to death and immortality for I want room to grow up in.' She lived in the reality of the eternal life of God and was therefore, in a sense, deathless. To be free from the fear of death is freedom indeed, since it is one of the greatest personal fears.

Then Paul takes up something else that might separate us from the love of God: 'life'. Death may be distant, but life is always with us. Some welcome death because they see it as an escape from bad circumstances. We need a strength and resilience not only to stand up to life, but to be more than a conqueror in it. This we also find in Jesus. Life may hold unnamed fears for many people and some get up in the morning saying to themselves wearily, 'Oh Lord, another day.' They begin the day overcome and end it in the same way. If this is you, try to remember that life holds nothing which Jesus has not overcome. Every morning when we wake, there is available a reservoir of hope and strength to face whatever the day holds. So, together with Jesus, we can say, 'Oh Lord, another day... to live for You.'

FURTHER STUDY

Acts 20:22–24;
1 Thess.
4:13–18

1. Why did Paul not fear life's hardships?

2. Why can we be encouraged in the face of death?

Lord God, I see that nothing need make me fearful. Help me to hold on to Your strength and receive Your hope this new day. How glad I am that through Your Spirit I am ready for anything and can do whatever needs to be done. Amen.

Seeing good as evil

FOR READING & MEDITATION – EPHESIANS 1:3–23

'far above all rule and authority, power and dominion' (v21)

Now we consider another thing that cannot separate us from the love of God: 'angels' (Rom. 8:38). Why did Paul say 'angels'? Would angels really want or try to separate us from the love of God? Paul has in mind here that angels represent the powers that are good. Absolutely nothing – good or bad – can come between us and God's love.

Surprisingly and interestingly, some people have been more afraid of good things than bad things. Why good things? They had such low self-worth and were so down on themselves that

FURTHER STUDY

Phil. 4:10–13;
Luke 10:17–20;
1 Tim. 6:6–18

1. Why should we not fear demons?

2. What secret did Paul share?

they could not conceive that they were worthy of receiving good things and enjoying the strength and positive sense of worth. They were therfore unable to experience good things positively. It has been said, 'No one is safe until he or she can stand anything that happens to them – good as well as bad.' It is important for us to know how to handle the good things as well as the bad and make them serve. It's important to be able to handle both prosperity and hardship if we are to live well.

Next on Paul's list comes 'demons'. There ought to be no doubt in anyone's mind that demons are present in the universe. Some Christians do not believe in their existence, but this attitude is unscriptural. Demons exist – the Bible says so. Others go to the opposite extreme and seem to see them everywhere. They see demons as being the cause of every problem and every difficulty. The balanced view is: demons exist, but they come under the control of Jesus. No demon, however bold or strong, can separate a Christian from God's love. Every one of them is on a leash. And the leash is in the nail-scarred hands of the one who engineered their defeat at Calvary.

Father God, help me to lay everything at Your feet – the prosperity as well as the difficulty, the joy as well as the sorrow. In Jesus' name I pray. Amen.

How never to be old

FOR READING & MEDITATION – ISAIAH 46:1–13

*'Even to your old age and grey hairs...
I am he who will sustain you.' (v4)*

In the list of things that cannot separate us from the love of God Paul then mentions 'neither the present'. It is difficult to know what Paul had in mind when he wrote these words, but it's likely he meant 'things as they are'. For some, life takes on a dull, monochrome grey colour and this gives them a monochrome outlook.

However, life in Jesus releases us from the tyranny of monotony. There is a creativity in Christ that puts a sparkle into life and makes it creative amid the uncreative. Things present do not have a hold because you do not belong to them; you belong to Jesus Christ. You receive the creative Spirit of Christ, and you are able to make all things serve.

After 'the present' Paul adds 'the future'. Millions are afraid of the future. Perhaps the most difficult aspect of the future for many is the idea of growing old. We all need to learn how to grow older, just as we teach young children how to grow up. For some the changes of retirement, for example, can be overwhelming for those who are not mentally or emotionally prepared for it. Dr Martin Gumpert, in his book *You are Younger Than You Think*, says that 'idleness is the greatest enemy of the aged and presents them with their ticket to death.' Michelangelo was writing poetry and designing buildings up to the time of his death at 89. Many people have done their finest work in their more mature years. Let's never retire from life. If you have to give up your work, look to take up new interests or revive old ones. If those interests can serve the kingdom of God, then all the better. Because of the Word become flesh, we can really live life to the full – whatever our age.

FURTHER STUDY

Psa. 92:12–15;
Rom. 8:18;
Gal. 1:3–4

1. What may we expect in old age?

2. How did Paul view the present?

Father God, I am thankful for the years that come and go, and, above all, I am thankful for the possibility that they can grow more beautiful and blessed. Amen.

Trouble with authority?

FOR READING & MEDITATION – MARK 12:1–17

'Give back to Caesar what is Caesar's and to God what is God's.' (v17)

Continuing our study of Paul's list of things that do not have the power to separate us from the love of God, we come to 'nor any powers' (Rom. 8:38). Here again, we do not know precisely what Paul was thinking about, but most probably he had in mind the powers that are over us in authority – a political power, for example, or even a dominant person.

There will be some reading these lines who have to live out their lives day after day under a totalitarian regime. They are able to endure this kind of tyranny because inwardly they have made the choice to be accountable to a higher power. Surrendered to the supreme authority – the kingdom of God – they are free amid any form of tyranny, because they are inwardly and spiritually free. The 'powers' have lost their power over them. 'I have the power to put you to death,' said a cruel ruler to a Christian who was arrested and charged with preaching the gospel, 'and I am going to use it.' 'But I have the power to die triumphantly,' responded the Christian. There is no doubt in my own mind who had the greater power.

FURTHER STUDY

Psa. 8:1–9;
John 19:1–11

1. What did the psalmist affirm?

2. How did Christ view Pilate's authority?

Then the next point: 'neither height'. Paul is thinking here, of course, of never being able to rise to a height where we can get beyond God's loving reach. The psalmist expressed a similar thought when he said, 'Where can I go from your Spirit? Where can I flee from your presence? If I go up to the heavens, you are there' (Psa. 139:7–8). The psalmist knew nothing of manned space probes with the potential to reach other planets, but that makes no difference. God's love spans the whole of creation; there is absolutely nowhere where His love cannot reach us.

Father, I see that 'the powers that be' lose their power over me when I am held by Your power. Your Word tells me to be subject to authority, but You want me to acknowledge Your authority as the highest – and this I do gladly. Amen.

God's love never fails

FOR READING & MEDITATION – JUDE 3–25

'keep yourselves in God's love' (v21)

The thought with which we ended yesterday is that God's love spans the whole of creation – there is simply nowhere where it is not. The opposite of 'height' is 'depth', and this is where Paul takes us now: 'neither height nor depth' (Rom. 8:39). Paul is highlighting here that just as we can search the highest heavens and never fail to find the love of God, so also is it with the depths. However far we descend into the depths, God's love has gone lower still.

I once met a submarine commander who told me that he had found Christ at the bottom of the sea. 'I was lying on my bunk in a submarine on a three-day exercise at the bottom of the ocean,' he said. 'I lifted my heart upwards to God in a prayer of repentance and I was saved that instant.' He smiled as I put my arm around him and said, 'neither height nor depth'.

Some commentators apply this thought of the 'depths' to the depths of depression. Though I do not think that is what Paul had in mind, it can certainly be applied to that. Do you struggle with depression? Then try to hold on to this: God's love reaches even there.

Finally Paul adds, 'nor anything else in all creation'. This covers all the things that have not been specifically mentioned. Nothing, absolutely nothing in the whole universe, can separate us from the love of God in Christ Jesus. We have perfect security as we give ourselves to His love.

This great passage of Paul's amazes us with its promises and its provisions. The decks are swept of possible failure and we stand on them 'more than conquerors'. There are many uncertainties in life, but we can be sure of this: God's love never fails.

FURTHER STUDY

Jonah 2:1–10; Rom. 8:35–39

1. What was Jonah's experience of God's reach?

2. Why can nothing separate us from God's love?

My Father and my God, Thank You that You are consistent and steady and that life holds nothing which can separate me from Your love. I have taken hold of this truth; now let it take hold of me. In Jesus' name. Amen.

Resources for you and you

After some of the unprecedented challenges faced all over the world this year, perhaps many of us have been reflecting on the meaning and importance of wellbeing, in our lives and in our churches. Now that we are starting to look ahead to another new year, this is a great time to consider how to invest in your walk with God, and in your own spiritual, mental and emotional wellbeing, throughout 2021. God cares deeply for us, and that includes all aspects of our lives.

We have two series that you, your small group or your whole church can engage with to help you live well, place God at the centre, experience His *shalom* peace and goodness and the impact this has on every aspect of our wellbeing.

These Three Things and **God's Plan for Your Wellbeing** are based on sound biblical teaching around how we have been designed to depend on God to meet our every need, and that He longs to meet those needs for us. Each has been developed with an abundance of additional resources available online, including sermon outlines, small group discussion starters and videos, to enable you to really get the best out of the teaching, whether through face-to-face or virtual learning.

These Three Things

Mick Brooks, CWR

God's plan for us is to live in relationship with Him, and look to Him as the primary source of our security, self-worth and significance. Because we are made in His image, only He can satisfy our deepest longings. Through 42 daily readings, explore how we can know life in all its fullness, even when things go wrong.

PROVISONAL COVER

God's Plan for Your Wellbeing

Dave Smith, Kingsgate Church

In this brand-new series, created with both Christians and sympathetic enquirers in mind, Dave Smith follows the wellbeing narrative of the Bible, and explores how when we discover God's plan for our wellbeing, we experience fuller understanding of His care and concern for the physical, spiritual, emotional, vocation, relational and financial areas of our lives.

For prices and to purchase, visit **cwr.org.uk/store**
For more information on how to register your interest and plan to engage your groups or churches in either of these series, visit **cwr.org.uk/for-your-church**

The basis of certainty

FOR READING & MEDITATION – 2 TIMOTHY 1:1–18

'For the Spirit God gave us does not make us timid, but gives us power, love and self-discipline.' (v7)

If, as we have been exploring, the Christian life is the conquest of life by *Life*, it's important to understand the grounds for drawing this conclusion. The verse chosen for today's text is one that will help to enlighten us. Listen to the way in which the Amplified Bible words it: 'For God did not give us a spirit of timidity (of cowardice, of craven and cringing and fawning fear) but [He has given us a spirit] of power and of love and of calm *and* a well-balanced mind *and* discipline *and* self-control'. Here, then, is our basis of being 'more than a conqueror': the whole person is strengthened. The will, our emotions, and mind are all renewed. There is strength for the will, love for the emotions, and sound judgment for the mind. What more could one want in order to cope with life?

FURTHER STUDY

Rom. 8:11–17; Gal. 5:22–25

1. What have we received?

2. What happens when we allow the Holy Spirit to help us?

When the will, emotions and mind are under the influence of Jesus then all fear is diminished. People attempt to overcome fear in many different ways. Some believe fear comes from an evil spirit and so try to cast it out. Others consider fear as being a purely psychological problem and try to educate it out. However, fear diminishes as it is displaced by someone greater who possesses you, thereby putting the fear into perspective. And that someone who comes alongside us to help us is none other than the third person of the Trinity – the Holy Spirit – who as our counsellor and comforter works to ease our fears and anxieties and to make known the presence of our Father in heaven.

When we learn how to strengthen the will, gain love for our emotions, and sound judgment for the mind, we are on the way to real living. It is the answer of Life to inadequate life.

Father, I see that it's too hard to overcome anything outside of me if You do not overcome everything inside of me. I invite You into my will, my emotions and my mind. Take them all and recreate them in the image of Your Son. Amen.

Fear – the thing to fear

FOR READING & MEDITATION – JEREMIAH 30:1–17

'So do not be afraid... do not be dismayed' (v10)

Before discovering how we can allow the Holy Spirit to work within us so that the paralysing fears are dissolved, we spend a few days looking at fear in an attempt to understand it more fully.

Is anything quite as prevalent as fear and anxiety? It must be recognised right away that some fears contribute to our safety and wellbeing. Fear, after all, is the best policeman on our busy roads. Driving through a wood one night, I surprised a deer, and immediately it bounded out of my way towards safety. The deer was extremely frightened. But its fear caused it to run from danger and helped preserve its life. I remember when my mother had a minor operation, and the nurses told her she was too calm. Medical research apparently had shown that those who show no fear take longer to recover from an operation. Some fear can be beneficial.

The fears and anxiety I am concerned with here, however, are the fears that paralyse us and incapacitate us. I can never forget a wildlife film I once saw which showed a small bird sitting on the branch of a tree being mesmerised by the eyes of a large cobra. It sat there crouched in fear before the cobra's overarching hood. Fear had paralysed it and made it easy prey.

We all need to learn how not to be paralysed by fear. Aware of it perhaps, even apprehensive, but never its prey. Some of our fears may well be of very real and present circumstances which tower over us like a cobra's hood and cause us great anxiety. Or they may be vague, inward, more intangible fears, like fear of failure, fear of poverty, fear of death, fear of illness, or fear of people. Whatever the fear, if it hinders our relationship with God and others, God wants to help us overcome it.

FURTHER STUDY

Isa. 43:1–7;
Matt. 14:25–33

1. Why need we not fear?

2. Why did Peter sink?

God my Father, whatever fears may be distressing me, give me Your power to be able to stand up to them – fearless and unafraid. In Jesus' name I ask it. Amen.

The road to overcoming

FOR READING & MEDITATION – MATTHEW 25:14–30

'So I was afraid and went out and hid your gold in the ground.' (v25)

The text we looked at two days ago – 2 Timothy 1:7 – reveals that God has not given us 'a spirit of timidity (of cowardice, of craven and cringing and fawning fear)' (Amplified). So where, then, does this timid spirit come from?

At the beginning of the twentieth century many psychologists believed we come into the world with just two fears – the fear of falling and the fear of loud noises. But by the time we reach adulthood, they said, we have gathered dozens more on the way. The science of prenatal psychology claims, however, that babies can come into the world with many fears, such as fears picked up from the mother as they lie in the womb. Others say that the devil is directly responsible for some fears. He either breathes them directly into the soul or exaggerates the fears already there.

FURTHER STUDY

Matt. 26:47–56;
John 20:19–20

1. What does fear cause us to do?

2. What does Jesus do when we hide in fear?

One story from Asia tells of a traveller who crossed a desert. As he did so he met a traveller coming from the opposite direction who identified himself as Cholera. 'Where have you come from?' asked the first traveller. Cholera named the city he had just left. 'How many died?' the traveller enquired. 'Eighty thousand,' Cholera replied, 'but I touched only 20,000.' 'And the rest?' 'Oh, they died from fear.'

The parable we have read today tells us about a man whose usefulness was diminished because of fear. How many Christians, I wonder, will go out into the world today and fail to increase the spiritual investment which Jesus has deposited within them because of some incapacitating fear? Fear so often paralyses us and prevents us serving Jesus. We need to find the strength and resilience over all our fears. Can it be done? Yes, thank God!

Father, the thought that I can be 'more than a conqueror' and overcome fear and anxiety gives me great hope. Teach me how to take the first steps on this road to overcoming fear. And teach me, also, to walk on it for ever. Amen.

What compels us?

FOR READING & MEDITATION – 2 CORINTHIANS 5:11–21

'For Christ's love compels us, because we are convinced that one died for all' (v14)

Because fear is possibly the greatest obstacle to entering into the experience of all that God wants for us, we continue our exploration of how it arises and what it does to the personality.

Some of our fears find roots in trauma and distress. The mind, wanting to forget the unpleasant, drops the incident that caused the distress down into the unconscious mind and closes the door on it. Sometimes, if the emotional content surrounding the unpleasant event is strong, it continues to work in the unconscious, causing tension and anxiety. The late great Dr Leslie Weatherhead, a Methodist minister who pastored the City Temple in London, told the story of an officer during the First World War, who would stand on top of a trench rather than get down into it. Some thought it was bravery, but the truth was he was paralysed by fear – fear of being in an enclosed space. Later, during therapy, it was discovered that when he was a child he was attacked in a narrow alley by a fierce dog – an event that left him with a fear of enclosed spaces.

FURTHER STUDY

Matt. 26:69–75;
Mark 7:24–30

1. How did fear affect Peter?

2. What compelled the woman to argue with Jesus?

It has to be said that many of us carry all kinds of repressed fears in our unconscious mind, but these fears rarely hinder us from functioning in life except, perhaps, on rare occasions. What is to be done with these fears? If they do not have any disabling impact upon us – nothing. The fears that have to be dealt with are those which paralyse us in life and create obstacles and obstructions in our relationships. When fear stops us being who we are in Jesus that fear needs to faced and brought into the light of His presence. As Christians we are to be compelled, not by fear, but by love.

Lord God, no longer do I need to be driven by fear when You are my Redeemer. Take from within me all basis of fear and fill me with Your love. This I ask in the gracious and conquering name of Jesus. Amen.

Pull out all the stops!

FOR READING & MEDITATION – 1 JOHN 4:7–21

'There is no fear in love. But perfect love drives out fear' (v18)

To be 'more than a conqueror' is easy to say, but how does it work out in day-to-day life? How can we learn to live a life that is free from paralysing fears and anxieties? First, by recognising and facing the things of which we are afraid. Denial simply does not work.

Next, to understand that many of our fears are rooted in one thing – inner division. The inwardly united personality, that of a person whose will, emotions and mind are held in the grip of Jesus, need not be paralysed by fear.

FURTHER STUDY

John 15:12–13;
Eph. 3:14–19

1. Why may some willingly die?

2. What did Paul pray for?

Answers to fear have been presented to the world by countless philosophers and social commentators and includes advice like: 'Restrict your desires, don't expect too much. Contract the area of your expectations and then life will not hit you on such a wide front. Thus your fears will be lessened.' This remedy for fear is: pull in. Gandhi, world leader and political ethicist said, 'Stand inwardly aloof, without desire for the fruit of action.' This remedy for fear is: pull apart. When Jesus is at the centre of our lives then the answer lies in our text for today, which in the Amplified Bible reads: 'There is no fear in love [dread does not exist], but full-grown (complete, perfect) love turns fear out of doors *and* expels every trace of terror'.

The answer, then, is not to pull in, nor to pull apart, but to pull out. Pull out all the stops! Expand your personality through perfect love so that love empowers the will, energises the emotions and clears the mind. This expansion drives out all fear. It turns it out of doors! The answer of the gospel is in line with its own nature – it is positive, affirmative, revolutionary and expansive.

My Father and my God, what would I give to live life without any paralysing fears? Yet all I need to give is myself. You have given Yourself unreservedly to me. Help me to give myself unreservedly to You. In Jesus' name I pray. Amen.

Unafraid!

FRI
27 NOV

FOR READING & MEDITATION – GENESIS 3:1–19

'I heard you in the garden, and I was afraid because I was naked; so I hid.' (v10)

Yesterday we said that fears are rooted in one thing – inner division. It follows, then, that one response to fear lies in a unified self – a self made whole by Christ. Perfect love literally does cast out fear just as, vice versa, imperfect love literally allows fear into the heart.

Before sin came into the world, Adam was a whole person who enjoyed the free flow of God's *agape* love. But when he listened to the tempter's lies and declared his independence from his Creator, he put up a barrier to that love, and the first thing that swept into his heart was fear. Notice his words: 'I was afraid.' When love fills our life, there is no room for fear; but when fear takes control, love is stifled.

**FURTHER
STUDY**

Jer. 31:1–6;
Heb. 4:14–16

If you follow what I am saying then you will discover one way to expel all unhealthy and paralysing fears. It begins and ends with love. But first, that love contracts. It narrows love down to one man – Jesus. One translation of 2 Corinthians 5:14, the verse we looked at the other day – 'For Christ's love compels us' – says this: 'The love of Christ narrows us.' We become single-minded, with one consuming passion that consumes the lesser passions of life. That does not mean we have no love for others, but that our love for others is fed by our love for Jesus. Certainly, we love others better when we love Him better.

1. Why is God's love perfect?

2. What can we do with confidence?

The love we receive from God fuses the divisions of the soul into a burning unity and our inner fears and anxieties are consumed. Fears find it hard to stay alive in this fire of love – His love provides a resilience that enables us to feel and face anything that life can send our way.

Lord Jesus, who conquered everything, I invite You now into my inner being, for when I am overcome by You then I can overcome anything. May my love for You increase day by day. For Your own dear name's sake. Amen.

'Listen to Him!'

FOR READING & MEDITATION – MATTHEW 17:1–13

'Jesus… said, "Don't be afraid." When they looked up, they saw no one except Jesus.' (vv7–8)

We are beginning to understand that it's difficult to fully overcome fear when there remains an inner tension or division. This is vividly brought home to us in the transfiguration scene. The Jewish heart of Peter was divided in its loyalty – wanting to keep Moses representing the law, Elijah representing the prophets, and Jesus representing the new revelation. He wanted them all to be on the same level. 'If you wish, I will put up three shelters,' he said, 'one for you, one for Moses and one for Elijah' (v4). In his enthusiasm, Peter's comment reveals that he lacked insight, for the whole of the future was bound up with the question of whether Jesus was the fulfilment of all that Moses and Elijah represented, and whether ultimate allegiance should be given to Him.

FURTHER STUDY

Psa. 19:1–7;
Heb. 1:1–3

1. How has God spoken to us?
2. What is different about Jesus?

Even while Peter was saying these words, a cloud overshadowed them and God's voice said, 'This is my Son, whom I love… Listen to him!' (v5). God could not have been more clear in announcing that Jesus was not on a par with Moses and Elijah; He was in a class all by Himself. Why were Peter and the other disciples so afraid? We read, 'When the disciples heard this, they fell face down to the ground, terrified' (v6). Their fear, I suspect was primarily brought about because they heard God's voice, but I think there was also the fear that came from inner division. When Jesus is not central then fear arises – inevitably.

God's voice is speaking to us today as surely as it did on the transfiguration mount, and it is saying the same thing: 'This is my Son, whom I love… Listen to him!' Believe me, fears will remain until we learn to listen to and hear God's voice above all the other voices that clamour for our attention.

Lord God, You are speaking today in response to our inner divisions. You are trying to show us that Jesus is the only one who can save us. Forgive us if we doubt or deny it. Help me to listen to Your voice above all others. Amen.

The greatest pain

FOR READING & MEDITATION – ROMANS 8:9–17

'The Spirit you received does not make you slaves, so that you live in fear again' (v15)

In some ways, conquering fear is relatively simple, although working through the resolutions requires something that many may find difficult. This includes becoming single-minded with one overriding desire that consumes the lesser desires of life. The more we allow Jesus' love to fill our personalities, the more our hearts are free from inner fears and anxieties and the confusion that comes from inner division.

It is my conviction that one of the greatest pains in the personality is the pain we experience when we do not feel loved. And because this is one of the greatest pains, one of the greatest fears is the fear of being unloved. Now nothing can dispel that deep insecurity except a genuine assurance that we *are* loved. And here the gospel comes in with just that assurance – and not simply the written assurance given by words in a book, but the vital assurance of the Word become flesh. That love was shown in the only way possible – in loving deeds to good and bad alike, and by the final act of Jesus Christ giving Himself for us on the cross. Now we know for certain that God loves us not because we are deserving and worthy, but because He can do nothing else but love. There is nothing we can do to earn His love, and nothing in us can extinguish it. He loves, full stop.

When we grasp that assurance then the fear of not being loved is an impossible fear, for we are loved no matter what we do or become. Now here's the problem: most Christians have grasped this truth, but it has not grasped them. They understand it, but they have not learned to stand upon it. Its strength is found in getting it from our heads into our heart.

FURTHER STUDY

John 14:25–26; 16:7–15

1. What would the Holy Spirit do for the disciples?

2. Why was it good for the disciples that Jesus was going away?

Father, I see that one of the greatest pains we can feel – the pain of being unloved – need never be mine. Help me get this truth into the central stronghold of my heart. In Jesus' name I pray. Amen.

Where love starts

FOR READING & MEDITATION – ROMANS 5:1–11

'God demonstrates his own love for us in this: while we were still sinners, Christ died for us.' (v8)

We are looking at how love drives out fear, and perfect love drives out all fear (1 John 4:18). Now this is not what we might expect. Usually when you hear a talk on how to conquer fear you might hear the speaker say something along these lines: 'The way to overcome fear is by confronting it with your faith.' There is some truth in that. But John, in his epistle, gets right to the root of the issue when he tells us that the most effective remedy for fear is love. If he had said, 'There is no fear in faith,' we would have had only half an answer, and we would try to match our faith against fear. But, as we said, probably our greatest fear is the fear of not being loved, and only Love – love with a capital L – can resolve that.

FURTHER STUDY

Luke 23:39–43;
Eph. 2:1–10

1. Why would a criminal go into paradise?

2. What was God's motivation to save us?

Faith has an important place in the Christian life, but we are now talking about the basics of living, and the basics of living are condensed into that one word: love. In reality, faith is a by-product of love – a result of the invitation of divine love into our hearts. The moment we begin to receive God's love, that moment we begin to love with His love. We love God with the love of God. And we love others with the love of God. God has loved us into loving, and into loving with His love.

When we begin to live in the truth that God loves us regardless, then that love produces love in us in return: 'We love because he first loved us' (1 John 4:19). It is not our love for Him that drives away fear, but His love for us. That love awakens love in us, and we begin to love in response – we begin to love Him and love others. His love generates love in you. This is the heart of our faith. Miss this, and you may miss your way.

Loving heavenly Father, help me to open my whole being to Your love. You love me without limit; may I likewise love others without limit. In Jesus' name. Amen.

Perfect Gifts for Christmas...

Advent

Unexpected Jesus

God's people had been waiting for a Messiah for as long as they could remember, but when He arrived, He wasn't quite what they had expected. Spend each day of Advent reflecting on how Jesus transformed lives in unexpected ways. Ideal for individual or small group use.

By Anna Robbins
ISBN: 978-1-78951-258-8
£6.99

Advent Together

Journey through *Advent Together* as a family, with daily Bible readings, thoughts and activities for the everyone to enjoy. Take a look at Old Testament prophecies about Jesus, and how we can prepare to celebrate His birth.
By Steve and Bekah Legg
ISBN: 978-1-78951-265-6
£8.99

Family Devotionals

More 12-week family devotionals from the Legg family. The four titles can be read in any order.

All Together
ISBN: 978-1-78259-692-9

Time Together
ISBN: 978-1-78259-798-8

Life Together
ISBN: 978-1-78259-999-9

Growing Together
ISBN: 978-1-78951-264-9
£8.99 each

For children and young people

NEW

The Camel Who Found Christmas
The littlest camel is concerned about going to see the new king who has been born. However, on the journey he learns from Mama Camel that everyone is big enough, everyone is important enough, everyone is smart enough and everyone is special enough to meet King Jesus.
By Alexa Tewkesbury
ISBN: 978-1-78951-273-1
£1.99

50 Christmasiest Bible Stories
With colourful cartoons and his unique style of storytelling, Andy Robb brings some of the Christmasiest Bible stories to life.
By Andy Robb
ISBN: 978-1-78259-418-5
£5.99

Ideal for ages 10–14

One You, One Year
These one-year devotionals are packed with inspiring Bible readings, relevant thinking points and life changing prayers. Written in an engaging and upbeat style with specific themes, these books will encourage young people in their walk with God.

One You, One Year: 365 for Boys
ISBN: 978-1-78259-994-4

One You, One Year: 365 for Girls
ISBN: 978-1-78259-993-7
£9.99 each

For women and men

Gifts for women

Unwavering

Jen Baker explores the power of living an intentional life, and how we can make decisions boldly and confidently when we remember who we are in Christ. An encouraging and thought-provoking read for women of all ages.

By Jen Baker
ISBN: 978-1-78951-247-2
£8.99

The Beauty Within

For women of all ages, this interactive, reflective journal considers how God sees us as His daughters, and how we can cultivate an inner beauty that reflects His image.

By Rosalyn Derges
ISBN: 978-1-78259-832-9
£12.99

Gifts for men

The Code

Written by the team at Christian Vision for Men, this is a 12-point honour code for today's Christian man to live by, and respond to the call to live an uncompromised, Jesus-centred life.

By Carl Beech, Nathan Blackaby and Ian Manifold
ISBN: 978-1-78951-149-9
£8.99

NEW

Or order by post – see order form on last page

Christian living

Provisional cover

NEW

NEW

Specks and Planks

Jeff Lucas is back with another collection of touching, funny and profound stories from his years of following Jesus. These short but heart-warming anecdotes bring a disarming level of insight to everyday experiences, causing you to ponder, laugh and see life through new eyes.

By Jeff Lucas

ISBN: 978-1-78951-244-1

£8.99

God's Plan for Your Wellbeing

Drawing lessons from the life of Elijah, church leader Dave Smith looks at how we can go back to God's plan for our physical, spiritual, mental, emotional, relational, vocational and financial wellbeing. With additional free material available online, this book makes a great resource for churches and small groups to journey through together.

By Dave Smith

ISBN: 978-1-78951-279-3

£8.99

Multi-buy
offers
available

One burning message

FOR READING & MEDITATION – GALATIANS 2:11–21

*'I have been crucified with Christ and I no longer live,
but Christ lives in me.' (v20)*

Yesterday we ended with the statement, 'Miss this, and you may miss your way.' When saying this I was referring to the truth that it is not our love for Jesus that dispels our fear, but His love for us.

Once, when I was being interviewed on a radio programme in Australia, I was asked this question: 'If you had a direct line into every church in the world, and you could send a message across that line to every church simultaneously – and in no more than 50 words – what would it be?' I did not have any hesitation before replying, and you may have read of me saying it before: 'If you think your problem is that you do not love God enough, then think again, for you have got it the wrong way round. The issue is much more likely you don't know how much God loves you.' Love begins and continues in the Christian heart when we allow His (*agape*) love to fill ours and create the same degree of (*agape*) love in us.

Many years ago, a missionary arrived in China. As she was being taken in a rickshaw through the crowded streets of the place where she was to live, a feeling of distress came over her. 'Oh, God,' she cried, 'I don't think I can love these people. The only way I can love them is to have a clearer picture of how much You love me.' As she sat in the rickshaw her prayer was answered. A wave of divine love poured into her spirit. She saw in a new way how much she was loved by God, and almost immediately her outlook changed. Distress and fear were replaced by a kind-hearted love and concern. And for the rest of her days, she never stopped loving.

FURTHER STUDY

Phil. 1:1–11;
2 Thess. 1:1–4

1. What was Paul's prayer for the Philippians?

2. Why did Paul commend the Thessalonians?

My Father and my God, I am so thankful that I do not have to strive to love. I simply allow Your Love to love me into loving. Help me grasp this truth for I see that it is central to all living. In Jesus' name I pray. Amen.

An open heart

FOR READING & MEDITATION – 1 JOHN 3:1–20

'This is how we know what love is: Jesus Christ laid down his life for us.' (v16)

We are thinking that it is predominantly through perfect love, and not faith, that fear is driven out (see 1 John 4:18). This is sound psychology. If John had said, 'Perfect faith drives out fear', that would have put the spotlight on the person who is trusting. We might claim, 'I have faith, therefore I have no fear'. In love, however, I am not the centre of attention because by its very nature love makes someone outside of oneself the centre of attention. Fear is driven out by 'the expulsive power of a new affection'. Love delivers us from self-attention and causes us to turn our attention to others. Therefore love, not faith, is the primary resolution for fear. Never forget that although faith is vital, it is a by-product of love. You are rarely afraid of people you love; you are more afraid of people you don't love.

FURTHER STUDY

Luke 10:25–37;
1 Thess. 4:9–10

1. What was Jesus' teaching about love?

2. What was Paul's teaching about love?

Salvation Army Commissioner Samuel Brengle (1860–1936), said: 'I opened my heart to the love of God and He gave me such a blessing I never dreamed a man could have this side of heaven. Oh, how I loved. In that hour I knew Jesus, and I loved till it seemed my heart would break with love. I loved the sparrows. I loved the dogs. I loved the horses. I loved little [children] on the street. I loved the world.' Strengthened and empowered by such love there is no fear of anybody, anything, or any situation. When we are loved we are less afraid to attempt anything God wants us to do for Him.

The secret of Commissioner Brengle's passion is in the words, 'I opened my heart to the love of God'. God's love cannot come in unless we let it in. If only we would open our hearts more to the Lord and His love – what an amazing difference we would see.

Father, I realise I am not the spring of love, but its channel. However, in order to flow out, love first has to come in. Help me open myself more fully to the great Niagara of Your love. Now and always. Amen.

The reason for living

FOR READING & MEDITATION – REVELATION 1:1–20

'To him who loves us and has freed us from our sins by his blood' (v5)

Today we summarise what we have been saying about love being the source that resolves our fears and anxieties. When we do not open our hearts to God so that His love flows in, we will struggle to maintain a unified personality. I want to encourage you today to open yourself to God's love. And as you do, you will find your heart responding to His great love – loving in return.

Where there is little or no love for God there will be little or no love for life, because ultimately life has its real meaning when He is at the centre of it. When we do not love life we become afraid of it. There have been numerous studies, research projects and papers published documenting the effects of growing up in the absence of love. The result is an adult who is much more vulnerable to stress, depression and loneliness; they are even more susceptible to physical illness and struggle in their relationships. This takes us back to what we said at the beginning of this section of our meditations: that the personality is made up of the will, the emotions, and the mind, and they can work effectively only as the love of God permeates through them.

FURTHER STUDY

1 Cor. 13:1–13

1. Why is personal sacrifice for others insufficient?

2. What are the characteristics of pure love?

Remember – it is perfect love that drives out fear. And perfect love means the love of God. The more His love can flow into us, the more fear will be dispersed. An old song says, 'Love is my reason for living.' Without love our existence may feel pointless and uncertain, and with little hope and resilience to stand against and overcome life's great fears.

I hope now the text on which we have been focusing shines for you with a new brilliance: 'in all these things we are more than conquerors through him who loved us' (Rom. 8:37).

Father, one thing is certain – fear and love cannot coexist. I choose Your way, the way of love. Today I open my whole being to Your love. Fill me to overflowing. May Your love flow in until every fear is dispersed. In Christ's name. Amen.

Life creative

FOR READING & MEDITATION – JOHN 15:1–17

'If you remain in me and I in you, you will bear much fruit' (v5)

As we have been seeing, to be 'more than a conqueror' it is vital for us to receive and be filled with God's love. Matters such as faith, self-discipline, prayer, and the regular reading of the Scriptures play a part too, but underpinning it all is love – that self-giving *agape* love that reflects God's love.

The more God's love, as expressed in the life of Jesus, permeates our personalities, the more alive we become. The mind becomes keener and more creative, our emotions deeper and more sensitive, and our will more active and decisive. The whole of life becomes out-reaching. This is because love is creative, and when the love of God is the motivating energy of our personalities, the movement of our lives is also creative. When there is love there is always a plus, a margin, for somebody else. We have 'bread enough and to spare'.

FURTHER STUDY

2 Kings 4:8–17;
Col. 1:1–10

1. How did the woman express creativity?

2. What are we called to express?

When we give our lives to Christ, it might feel overwhelming, the thought and responsibility to be His representative to love others, and be kind to others. Things we thought ourselves incapable of tackling may feel all too much to take in and to take hold of. But Love – that is, divine love – provides the strength and the resilience that makes the whole of life creative.

If you allow the truths we have been uncovering during these past days to take a hold in your life then don't be surprised to find yourself thinking and acting creatively. A man known to me who felt that he lived a very monochrome and uncreative life came into a fresh experience in giving himself to Christ, and within weeks had started three new outreaches for youth in his church. Creative love flowed in and creative love flowed out.

Father God, how I thank You for the creative impact of Your love. Please help me be creative this day, wherever I am, and wherever I go may I bring Your light and life and peace into unrest and disorder. In Jesus' name I ask it. Amen.

Partners – **making a difference in times of crisis**

For 55 years now, thanks to the support of our Partners, Christians all over the world have been equipped to walk every day with Jesus. This year the world has been shaken on a global scale by the Covid-19 pandemic and none of us have been immune to its effects. Thank you so much all for your continued support through this difficult period, especially if you have faced personal struggles and loss. The impact of the prayers and financial support of CWR Partners is huge, making a difference to thousands of lives each day as people grow in their relationship with God despite their individual concerns.

Alan*, a former prisoner, says: 'While I was in prison, every issue of *Every Day with Jesus* spoke to me where I was emotionally and mentally at the time. I know now just how much God loves me despite my sin and rejection. It's opened my heart to feeling a love I've never felt before.'

Will you become a Partner and provide support to people just like Alan?

Just £15 a month will ensure that thousands of other prisoners just like Alan get their daily Bible reading notes to help transform, grow and sustain them.

Partners' support puts over 60,000 copies of *Every Day with Jesus* into the hands of prisoners each year.

Become a Partner TODAY – your support really does make a difference.

Please email **partners@cwr.org.uk** or,

to make a one-off donation, visit **cwr.org.uk/donate**

*Name changed for anonymity.

Love is...

FOR READING & MEDITATION – JOHN 7:25–39

'Whoever believes in me... rivers of living water will flow from within them.' (v38)

Yesterday we said that one of the issues underlying our ability to be 'more than a conqueror' is the need for our lives to be filled with God's love. And because love is creative, we become creative, and we look at life through creative eyes.

It is difficult to imagine a Christian who is living in vital contact with the One who created all things (Col. 1:16) going through any day without demonstrating some creativity. And this can take many different forms. 'The first thing I did when I fell in love with Jesus,' a woman once told me, 'was to redecorate my home.' She went on to say that prior to her conversion she had no interest in the way her home looked, but when Jesus came in His creativity prompted her into creativity. I am not suggesting that in order to prove our spirituality and that we are in touch with the creative Christ every one of us has to redecorate our home, dig the garden, or go out and start a new movement! What I am saying is this: because divine love is creative, we can expect hope and life and energy to be at work in our lives and be ready to give expression to it. It's astonishing how we go through task after task in the same old way when, with a little thought and creativity, the most ordinary of tasks can be done in different and more inventive ways.

FURTHER STUDY

Acts 9:36–41;
Titus 3:8

1. How did Dorcas express her love?

2. What should we devote ourselves to?

The creativity I am talking about here is not innate creativity, and I recognise that some have more of this than others. However, when we belong to the One who *is* love, and whose love spills over into creativity, then something of that will be imparted to us – if we let it. People who are loved are people who love, and love is nothing if not creative.

Father, Your love has impacted my life in the most creative way. Now may Your love flowing through me impact others in the same creative way. This I ask to the praise and glory of Your precious name. Amen.

Conquered – to conquer

FOR READING & MEDITATION – ACTS 20:13–38

'we must help the weak, remembering the words…
"It is more blessed to give than to receive."' (v35)

Another way in which the Word who lived among us changes our lives is by releasing us from a preoccupation with ourselves. People have often told me that each time an occasion arises when they could be of help to someone, they are stopped by their inhibitions – they think more of their own feelings than of those of the person in need.

A friend of mine once told me this story: 'I travelled from London to the South Coast, hoping to enjoy the scenery along the route, but my car gave me trouble all the way. It would go for a few miles then stop. I would tinker with it a bit and then it would go for a few more miles – and stop. I wanted to look at the scenery, but all my attention was focused on the engine which was functioning so erratically. Had the engine been right I could have forgotten it and concentrated on enjoying the view.' By the time he arrived at his destination he had a splitting headache. Little wonder!

In a similar manner, many of us can have our strength impaired and attention distracted by having our focus in the wrong places. This most often happens when we don't fully depend on God but try to remain in the driving seat. And even when we hand over the steering wheel we find it hard not to be a backseat driver. At the end of the day this will exhaust us, and we will have missed opportunities to serve others because our minds and hearts are locked in tension and anxiety.

To conquer, we must be conquered; to love, we are first loved; to serve, we are first served. All these things Jesus offers to do for us. When we let Him, then one of the inevitable results is that we are released from ourselves. What a release!

FURTHER STUDY

Matt. 25:31–45; Heb. 13:16

1. Why may we miss opportunities to minister to Christ?

2. What must we not forget?

Lord Jesus, You whose own concerns and struggles did not prevent You from reaching out to the many who crowded around You, please give me that strength too. Make me more and more like You. For Your own dear name's sake. Amen.

The unhurried heart

FOR READING & MEDITATION – ISAIAH 26:1–15

'You will keep in perfect peace those whose minds are steadfast, because they trust in you.' (v3)

A further consequence of Jesus dwelling at the centre of our life is that we will know what it is to have an unhurried heart. Jesus approached life responsibly, passionately, decisively, but also with a calm and confident spirit. Comb the Gospel records and never once do you find Him in a hurry. One commentator said this about Jesus: 'He was never hurried, never flurried and never worried.' He was busy, focused, and travelled a good deal, but He always had time for people and their needs. His strength was in that whatever the circumstances or situations He faced, He constantly sought His Father's guidance and trusted Him with every detail of His life.

FURTHER STUDY

John 14:1,27; Heb. 4:1–11

1. What is Jesus' legacy?

2. Who can experience God's rest?

There can be little doubt that the trusting heart is the unhurried heart. Trust is one of those words which trips readily off our tongues, but so few of us know what it means to depend completely on God and trust Him fully – myself included. At one time, I used to think that my life was the very epitome of trust. But I realise as I look back that a lot of it was pretence or wishful thinking. Trust means believing God is holding one's life, and that He is constantly working to ensure His purposes are brought to pass – even through our mistakes and imperfections.

'Do you believe I can take you safely across a high wire in my wheelbarrow?' said Blondin, the tightrope walker, to a little boy who sat watching his act with amazement. 'Oh yes,' said the boy, 'of course I do.' 'Then get into the wheelbarrow,' invited Blondin. 'No fear,' was the reply. The boy believed – but only so far. Trust is believing all the way. And those who trust like that, experience the joy of the unhurried heart.

Lord Jesus, You moved through life with an unhurried heart. Give me that same confidence of spirit, that same degree of trust, so that I can start each day with my head held high and my heart at perfect peace. In Jesus' name. Amen.

Three types of Christian

FOR READING & MEDITATION – COLOSSIANS 3:1–17

'For you died, and your life is now hidden with Christ in God.' (v3)

Yet another consequence of the conquering Christ indwelling us is that we receive the strength to live 'in spite of'. Many of us have strength to live 'on account of', but not strength to live 'in spite of'.

When our circumstances and surroundings are favourable, and life is going according to plan, we can carry on. But life is not always like that. There can be huge disappointments, distressing situations and cruel reverses. And that is when we are tested to the very core of our being. If what we have is merely an echo of our surroundings then it fades away and disappears. If what we have comes from the depths within us – where our Jesus life resides – then it holds us safe and steady and secure.

One writer said that there are three types of Christians: the rowing boat type, the sailing boat type, and the engine-driven type. The rowing boat type is the person who makes a show of being a Christian but, when under test, prefers to rely on his or her own strength. The sailing boat type depends on the winds. If the winds are with them, they get on, but if not, they make no progress. The engine-driven type has a strength and resilience that is constant – they go on whether or not the winds are favourable. It is true they go faster when the wind is behind them but, nevertheless, they go on – wind or no wind. They are not self-dependent or circumstance-dependent, but God-dependent. And being God-dependent they are, in turn, dependable.

This strength to go on when life is against us is one of our greatest necessities. To those who understand what it means to be conquered by Christ's love, and have His power within, it is a working truth.

FURTHER STUDY

2 Cor. 1:8–11; 4:7–18

1. Why can we endure beyond our abilities?

2. Where should we focus our attention?

Jesus, my Saviour and my Lord, You kept going when life became so tough that it meant dying on a cross. Take hold of me so that I might know that same power also; the power to go on – 'in spite of'. Amen.

Power over every sin

FOR READING & MEDITATION – ROMANS 13:1–14

'do not think about how to gratify the desires of the flesh.' (v14)

We continue looking at some of the consequences of having the Word of God living within us. Another result of Jesus' indwelling is that we have an inner strength and resilience to resist sin.

One of the greatest difficulties to overcome in pastoral counselling, according to one survey, is the moral fatalism that says concerning our thoughts and actions: 'What could I do? I am just a human being like everyone else!' 'What choice did I have? I had no option.' The implication is that as long as we remain human we remain sinful, and there is very little that can be done about it. This way of thinking is a form of fatalism. If we are going to be 'more than conquerors', we need to understand that though we can never reach a point in this life where it is not possible to sin, we can have a relationship with Jesus Christ through which it becomes possible not to sin.

FURTHER STUDY

Rom. 6:1–23

1. Why can we have power over sin?

2. Contrast the terms 'wages of sin' and 'gift of God'.

The truth is, sin is an intrusion, an invader in the universe, for we were not designed to be sinning beings. It's a result of our declaration of independence, and choosing to step away from our only real source and supply of security, self-worth and significance. One theologian says: 'There are three unnatural things which have invaded life: sin, the unnatural evil of the soul; error, the unnatural evil of the mind; and disease, the unnatural evil of the body.' This is why salvation is often referred to as 'health'. To be 'saved' means to be 'whole'. Always keep this in mind: sin has been conquered. Do not be tempted to believe anything else. The verse chosen as our text for today shows us how we can prepare, not for failure, but to be more than a conqueror.

Father, no word of Yours has as much power as that which opens up for me the possibility of overcoming sin. Help me to be as free from sin as it is possible to be. In Jesus' name I pray. Amen.

Fighting! Fighting!

FOR READING & MEDITATION – MATTHEW 3:1–17

'He will baptise you with the Holy Spirit and fire.' (v11)

Another consequence of the conquering Christ dwelling within us is that much of the tension is taken out of life. At first this idea may seem close to the one we looked at three days ago – the unhurried heart – but, as you will see, there is a difference.

Many Christians live tense and stressed spiritual lives in the sense that they try too hard to be good. Their fists are clenched, their teeth set, their backs are to the wall – they are fighting, fighting, fighting. It is all very earnest, but not very inviting. This type of godliness is a stressed godliness, and people looking on say to themselves, 'If this is what Christianity is all about, it doesn't looking very attractive.' In addition, it is exhausting for the person who is living in this way. All strain means total drain.

A scientist, when visiting a tin-plate factory, was told that in one of the processes the inner strain was taken out of the plates by subjecting them to fierce and intense heat. After this process the molecules were so harmonised that, when the tin plates were bent, they would not break. Today's text tells us how Jesus would baptise not with water, but with the Holy Spirit and fire. Isn't this what we need? A fiery baptism that will purify and melt us and, in a sense, set the molecules of our souls in a right relation to each other so that when the pressures come upon us, we will not break, but only bend. Life is rarely broken from without; it is broken from within. The presence of this fire-baptising Jesus in our hearts is essential for inner stress, tension and strain to be taken away. And when our lives are so harmonised within, they can stand anything that happens without.

FURTHER STUDY

Rom. 8:1–14;
1 Pet. 1:6–9

1. How can the Spirit help us fight sin?

2. Why can fiery trials be good for us?

Lord Jesus, it is clear from everything I read about You in the Gospels that although You were put under pressure, You never broke. Please baptise me with fire, until all strain is taken out. Amen.

A double victory

FOR READING & MEDITATION – 1 CORINTHIANS 15:35–58

'But thanks be to God! He gives us the victory through our Lord Jesus Christ.' (v57)

Today we end our meditations on the theme 'more than conquerors'. Tomorrow we begin new mediations for the Christmas season. What, then, have we learned from Paul's stirring words, 'in all these things we are more than conquerors through him who loved us' (Rom. 8:37)? What strength and resilience for living can be ours?

I can summarise the formula for resilient living in one sentence like this: To be a conqueror in Christ we are first and foremost to be conquered by Christ. Those who do not allow themselves to be taken up by Christ and His love will find themselves lacking the unified personality that we discussed earlier. In the unified personality the will, emotions, and mind are fully immersed by Jesus and His love, and the reins of these otherwise wild and untamed 'horses' are put in His powerful hands. The real secret is to be so conquered by His love, so motivated by it, so infused by it, that all the heart's hostility is overwhelmed and all its suspicions and distrusts overpowered.

FURTHER STUDY

Eph. 4:17–32

1. What are we to put on and what to put off?
2. How should we handle anger?

Some old tribal rituals promote the belief that when one man conquers another, the strength of the one conquered passes into the conqueror. However ill-founded that belief, something like that does, in reality, happen to us spiritually. When we overcome something through Jesus, strength is gained from the conquest in two ways. First, it establishes the habit of success within us, making it easier to engage in the next struggle. This also means the more we conquer, the more we can conquer – through Jesus Christ. Second, by overcoming we are able to pass the encouragement on to others. And in passing it on, we become more secure ourselves. In a twofold way we become 'more than conquerors'.

Father, I'm beginning to see that I can never conquer anything outside of me until You have conquered everything inside of me. Again I ask You to give me inner strength and resilience so that I might enjoy outer life and vitality. Amen.

THE WORD
became flesh and blood,
AND MOVED
into the neighbourhood.

We saw
THE GLORY
with our own eyes,
the one-of-a-kind glory,
LIKE FATHER,
LIKE SON,

Generous
INSIDE and OUT,
true from start to finish.

John 1:14, *The Message*

'The great divide'

FOR READING & MEDITATION – JOHN 1:1–14

'The Word became flesh and made his dwelling among us.' (v14)

We turn our attention now during this season of Advent to exploring just how much life has changed because, as John so powerfully yet simply wrote in the words of today's text, 'The Word became flesh and made his dwelling among us' (John 1:14). Without doubt this is one of the most amazing truths found in Scripture. Bible commentator William Barclay said, 'It might well be held that this is the greatest verse in the New Testament.' E. Stanley Jones remarked, 'If I were asked to put my finger on the most important verse to be found anywhere in the Word of God I would unhesitatingly put my finger on this one.' This is the opinion of many other theologians and commentators also.

FURTHER STUDY

Matt. 1:18–23;
John 20:24–31

1. Why was Jesus given the name Immanuel?

2. Why did John write his Gospel?

Why should such a simple sentence be so highly valued? Because it is here that the uniqueness of Jesus and of the Christian faith is so strikingly summarised. The declaration, 'The Word became flesh' has been described as 'the great divide' because it separates the Christian faith from every other religion on earth. In all other religions the emphasis is on humanity's search for God; in Christianity the emphasis is on God's search for humankind. The gospel of Jesus is not merely a command, instructing us to do something, but a demonstration – revealing to us what God has done for us.

Let this truth astound you if you will: the One who is infinite became incarnate, the eternal one contained in time. Allow the wonder of it to settle in your spirit as we walk once again past the manger at Bethlehem. At that first Christmas over two thousand years ago, one of the greatest mysteries of the ages took place: God became a baby.

My Father and my God, though I am not able to understand all the implications of Your Son's incarnation, I know that what prompted it was Your eternal love. May my love be kindled afresh by the flame of Your love. In Jesus' name. Amen.

'Nothing to equal it'

FOR READING & MEDITATION – 1 TIMOTHY 3:1–16

'He appeared in the flesh... was preached among the nations, was believed on in the world' (v16)

Yesterday we began to explore the amazing truth found in the sentence, 'The Word became flesh' and how it is considered as the great divide that separates the Christian faith from every other religion on earth.

A missionary told of how, when he began his ministry in Asia, everything of the gospel he presented to the people was met with indifference: 'What you say is good, but we have something similar in our sacred books.' When he talked about Jesus and His teachings, sharing biblical truths on turning the other cheek or going the second mile, people would react by saying something like this: 'Our sacred books tell us we are to be like sandalwood, which, when smitten by an axe, pours its perfume upon the very axe that smites it.' When he talked about the sufferings of Christ on the cross they told him about the Hindu god Shiva who 'drank poison that we might ambrosia taste'. The missionary wondered to himself, 'How can I best help these people understand the person of Jesus?' Then it dawned upon him that one of the greatest differences between the Christian faith and other religions lies in the fact that God became a real human being. When he began to talk about the incarnation, he noticed that people's interest was aroused. Those who became Christians told him later, 'Our religion contains many words, but we have nothing to equal a Word become flesh.'

FURTHER STUDY

Heb. 2:10–18; 10:1–10

1. Why did God's Son become a human being?

2. What did God prepare for His Son?

'Nothing to equal a Word become flesh.' What an observation! This is what makes Christianity unique: it is a religion different from all the other religions. Many religions have a word with more words, but only Christianity has a Word become flesh and, as *The Message* paraphrase reads, 'moved into the neighbourhood'.

Father God, please help me gain a clearer understanding of who You are and how You have revealed Yourself to us in the person of Your Son. And give me a new appreciation of the wonder of Jesus' incarnation I pray. Amen.

The ladder

FOR READING & MEDITATION – GENESIS 28:10–22

'he saw a stairway resting on the earth, with its top reaching to heaven' (v12)

Today we think a little more about the statement with which we ended yesterday: 'Many religions have a word with more words, but only the Christian faith has a Word become flesh.' Let me try to make the meaning a little clearer.

In all other religions, the word (the articles of belief) is expressed through words that set out a path to follow. Those words break down into philosophies, systems, practices, and so on. The principles are conveyed in words. Only in Jesus did the Word become flesh – a person.

FURTHER STUDY

John 5:16–18;
1:45–51;
6:32–42;
10:25–39

1. What links heaven and earth?

2. Why did the Jews try to kill Jesus?

In schools and colleges in many countries around the world there are classes in 'comparative religions'. The teachings of the various religions are outlined and the parallels drawn out. In these classes the Christian faith can appear similar to other religions, and not unique. Some in a pluralistic society such as we have now in the United Kingdom may perhaps criticise me for saying this, but the Christian faith is not just different from other faiths, more liberating, more free from contradictory elements, more exciting in its concepts – it is fundamentally different in kind. It doesn't set out to show humankind how to extend a ladder up to God to attain salvation, rather it claims the ladder has been dropped down to us out of heaven, and that God Himself has come down that ladder in the person of His one and only Son.

What other religion has a message like this? Christianity is not just a good idea, but an idea become fact. Without this fact the Christian faith would have a word become word – a philosophy, a system. It has, however, a Word become fact – a redemptive fact lived out in the person of Jesus. Nothing but this can save us.

Lord Jesus, how can I put into words the amazement that is in my heart as I realise that because I could not climb up to You, You climbed down to me? I thank You and praise Your glorious name. Amen.

Why 'the Word'?

FOR READING & MEDITATION – 1 JOHN 1:1–10

*'which we have looked at and our hands have touched –
this we proclaim concerning the Word of life.' (v1)*

Today I would like us to reflect on the term 'the Word' and the way it is used of Jesus Christ. Scholars tell us the term 'the Word' was not used of an independent being in Hebrew thought. The Old Testament speaks of 'the word of the Lord', or 'your word', but not 'the Word' to describe a separate entity. The term *logos*, meaning 'word', was common in Greek thought, however, so the early Christian writers did not hesitate to reach out beyond their Hebrew heritage and take hold of a concept that was waiting to be adapted. John, at the beginning of his Gospel, when looking for a way of introducing us to Jesus Christ, fastens on to that familiar Greek word. Christ, he tells us, is the divine *Logos*, the divine Word. Why did he call Jesus 'the Word'?

Well, words are the expression of hidden thoughts. If I had just sat here at my computer and not put my thoughts into words, hoping you would catch my ideas intuitively and use them as a devotional incentive for the day, then you would at this moment be looking at a blank page. Only as hidden thoughts are put into words will they express meaning and, hopefully, contribute to your spiritual growth and development.

The hidden God, like hidden thought, cannot be comprehended by human minds unless He communicates Himself through a word. You cannot know God clearly by intuition alone, for your heart with its sin and cross-currents is an unsafe soil for the revelation of God. If we are to know His hidden thoughts, then He must reveal them to us in a word. Jesus is that Word – the Word that contains the full and final revelation of God. And not just verbal, but vital.

FURTHER STUDY

Matt. 11:11;
John 1:1–4;
Luke 1:13–17

1. Contrast Jesus and John.

2. Meditate on the implications of Jesus being called 'the Word'.

God my Father, much of You is hidden. I cannot always read Your intentions, so how could I know You unless You showed Yourself to me? In Jesus this is exactly what You have done. And I shall be thankful for all eternity. Amen.

The authentic Word

FOR READING & MEDITATION – HEBREWS 1:1–14

'He has spoken to us by his Son... through whom also he made the universe.' (v2)

We have emphasised that without a word the thought cannot be expressed. The word is the thought made clear to our understanding. When you have grasped my words, providing of course that my words are comprehensible, then you have grasped my thought. Please note, however, that my words are not a third thing standing between you and the thought; they are the thought made available. The word and the thought are one.

The hidden God expresses Himself through the Word made flesh. When you take hold of the Word made flesh you do not take hold of something standing between you and God. That Word – Jesus – is God made available. When you know Him, you know God. Just as the thought and the word are one, so are God and Jesus one. Jesus made this plain when He said, 'I and the Father are one' (John 10:30) and when He said to Philip, 'Anyone who has seen me has seen the Father' (John 14:9).

FURTHER STUDY

2 Cor. 4:4–6; Col. 1:15–23

1. How is the Son the image of God?

2. What dwelt in Christ?

The question is: Why did the Word have to become flesh? There are a number of answers we can give to that question, the first being this: God became flesh in order to reveal Himself more perfectly. But hasn't God revealed Himself in nature? Yes, but not perfectly, not fully. When we look up to God through nature alone, we may come to the conclusion that God is law, yet a very impersonal kind of law. The discovery of nuclear energy is said to have turned many scientists to thoughts about God. These scientists, when questioned about God, describe Him as awesome, powerful and dependable. But the full truth about God cannot be seen in the splitting of the atom. That tells us simply about His creativity. The full truth is found only in Jesus. In Him God unfolds both His creativity and His character.

Lord God, forgive us when we try to project our own thoughts into the heavens and call them Your revelation. Thank You that in Jesus we have an authentic Word – the Word that is greater than human words. Amen.

Imperfect media

FOR READING & MEDITATION – JOHN 6:41–59

'No one has seen the Father except the one who is from God' (v46)

Yesterday we saw that although God reveals Himself in nature, this revelation is not complete. But what about His revelation through the men and women of the Old Testament – the prophets, the judges and the teachers? Scripture tells us that these men and women were inspired by the Holy Spirit and so, despite the frailty and imperfection of their lives, the truth was passed on through them.

There is one point of sadness though – some of them seemed to contradict in their lives the truth that crossed their lips. King David is just one example. He was a 'man after [God's] own heart' (Acts 13:22), yet planned and committed two of the ugliest and most damaging sins – murder and adultery. The message was perfect, but often the channel through which the message came was imperfect.

There is also the matter of words. Words are wonderful tools to convey thought, but they too have their inadequacies and imperfections. Linguists tell us that words get their meaning from life. Think, for instance, of the word 'home'. To some that word will convey love, warmth, affection; to others, hostility or misery and shame. The word acquires its meaning from life's experiences. This is why the poet Coleridge said, 'Literature can never rise higher than life.' For life puts content and meaning into literature.

When we see words such as 'love', 'God' or 'purity' in a book, what do we do? We read into them our highest experience of those words. But our highest experience of love, for example, is not the highest love; our highest experience of love is partial and incomplete. We see love at its highest when we see it wrapped up in the life and ministry of Jesus.

FURTHER STUDY

Matt. 23:1–7;
1 Pet. 2:21–25

1. Why were the Pharisees imperfect?

2. Why was Christ perfect?

Father, I see only faintly whatever window I look through, except when I look at the life of Your Son. What I see in Him sets my heart on fire, and I long to behold more and more. Amen.

God's self-revelation

FOR READING & MEDITATION – JOHN 14:1–14

'Anyone who has seen me has seen the Father.' (v9)

We continue reflecting on the thought that words, though a powerful medium of communication, cannot express fully what God is like. The difficulty can be seen when we take a word such as 'God' and then read into it our highest understanding of that word. But our highest understanding of 'God' is not God. What, then, do we need for a perfect revelation of God? A life had to come among us – a divine life which would put fresh content into the words associated with God and lift them to a new and more meaningful level. Well, this has happened.

FURTHER STUDY

John 10:30–38;
12:44–46

1. Why are words inadequate to understand God?

2. How can we understand what God is like?

Two thousand years ago a life came down to us from heaven and lived among us. He showed us what God was really like and lived a life that demonstrated the divine nature in a way possible for us all to understand. Whenever we think now of the word 'love' we no longer need to see it in terms of our poor partial love, but in the light of a love that prayed for enemies upon a cross: 'Father, forgive them, for they do not know what they are doing' (Luke 23:34). Now when we reflect on the word 'God' we need not rely on our imagination. The nature of God has been uncovered in understandable terms – human terms. I look to God through Jesus and I now know more fully than I could through reading the Old Testament what God is like, because Jesus is a true likeness of His Father. He is a good God, a trustworthy God.

One theologian said, 'If God isn't like Jesus then I am not interested in Him.' A student who heard him, remarked, 'His words took my breath away.' We need not worry, however, that God is different from Jesus, because Jesus is God's authentic self-revelation. We see in Jesus God as He really is!

Son of God, thank You for showing us the Father. We would never have known fully what He was like had we not looked on Your face. Seeing Him in Your face we are satisfied. Our gratitude knows no bounds. Amen.

Jesus – 'God approachable'

FOR READING & MEDITATION – HEBREWS 2:1–18

'Since the children have flesh and blood, he too shared in their humanity' (v14)

There can be no doubt that we catch glimpses of the character of God in nature, in the lives of the saints, and so on. But if we are to see God – really see Him – then we see Him best in the person Jesus Christ. I love the phrase which I think was first coined by E. Stanley Jones, describing Jesus as 'God approachable'.

In the Old Testament Job once asked the question, 'Canst thou by searching find out God?' (Job 11:7, AV). What we find in our search for God is not necessarily God, but our ideas about Him. There is a tendency within us all to create God after our own image, in the image of our imagination. Philosophers have tried to find God through the medium of philosophy, but He is not to be found there. For centuries they have plied words upon words, but despite the multiplicity of their words they have not discovered the Word. Someone has flippantly defined philosophy as 'a blind man in a dark room looking for a black cat that isn't there'. Philosophic reasoning (not in itself something to be dismissed) has searched in a dark universe for a philosophical God who isn't there. One of the greatest nations for philosophical thought is India, but none of its philosophers ever imagined a God who is a Father. Neither did they conceive of a God who would take on a body and become like us in order to redeem us. A love like that just does not exist – at least in the categories of philosophy.

In the real world, however, seeing is believing; the Word who was God, and was equal with God, became flesh and dwelt among us. The Son of God became the Son of Man in order that the sons of men might become the sons of God.

FURTHER STUDY

Mark 10:13–16;
Heb. 10:19–22;
12:18–24

1. Why was Jesus indignant?
2. What do the two mountains signify?

My Father and my God, what an amazing message Christmas contains. It is not about us knocking at the door of heaven, but You knocking at the door of our hearts. What grace, what humility, what love! I am deeply, deeply thankful. Amen.

Jesus' kind of love

FOR READING & MEDITATION – JOHN 13:12–38

'A new command I give you: love one another.
As I have loved you' (v34)

One of the most dangerous temptations in the Church today is the movement away from the person of Christ to the principles of Christ.

Some time ago I watched a television programme in which a group of theological lecturers claimed that if we focus too much on Christ and not on His principles, then, when controversy rages around His person, the sound principles which He taught become devalued and overlooked. 'It's not about whether Jesus is the Son of God, or that He was born of a virgin,' said one of the lecturers, 'but whether His teaching enables us to live more effective lives.' When I heard that, I feared for the churches which will one day be led by the students of these lecturers. How we need to pray for revival in all our theological colleges where the Christian faith is being taught.

FURTHER STUDY

Rom. 5:6–11;
Eph. 4:31–5:2

1. Contrast human love and Christ's love.

2. How can we imitate God?

When we take the principles of the Christian faith and marginalise the person of Jesus Christ, then we take the stream but not the source, the rays but not the sun. Apart from the person of Christ the principles would mean something else. Take the text before us today for example: 'A new command I give you: love one another. As I have loved you, so you must love one another.' Without the last portion – 'As I have loved you, so you must love one another' – there would have been nothing new in the commandment. The principle of love which had been spelt out in the Old Testament takes on a new meaning when set against the backdrop of Christ's person. Jesus put a higher meaning into love by the way He loved. In every part of the universe the norm for love is Jesus' kind of love. Other kinds of love may be good, but not the best.

Father, it's sad when people seem to settle for the impersonal rather than the personal. Yet it is You the soul most deeply craves. May others come to know You as I know You. In Christ's name. Amen.

Principle or person?

FOR READING & MEDITATION – JOHN 10:1–21

'They... will listen to my voice, and there shall be one flock and one shepherd.' (v16)

We continue to explore the relationship between principles and the person. Advocates of spirituality may talk about God as a 'divine principle'. They may talk to themselves about God, but they cannot talk to God. You cannot talk to a principle – only to a person.

A religion founded on the 'divine principle' is a religion where you end up talking to yourself. Take a young child crying in the middle of the night and asking for its mother. What if someone came along to comfort them saying: 'Let me tell you about the principle of parenting. Parenting is a deep love and concern for one's children. It means being aware of their needs and attending to those needs even if it involves endless sacrifice. Parents are wonderful, and you ought to be glad about this principle because it will help you understand life. Now go back to sleep.' What do you think the child would say? 'I want my parents.'

We cannot say our prayers to a principle or worship an axiom. Once, when there was a general election in the UK, on the day when the votes were cast a television camera spotted a woman standing in front of a ballot box with her hands folded as if in prayer. It looked as if she was being very spiritual. Then an interviewer asked her what she was doing. 'I'm praying,' she explained, 'to the ballot box, for this is the god who decides things.' Prayers to a ballot box did not decide the outcome of the election; the number of votes placed in the box decided it. Prayer and worship are the response of a person to the one who is known by the name of the Good Shepherd. Again I say it: there can be no communion with a divine principle – only with a divine person.

FURTHER STUDY

1 Cor. 1:4–9;
1 John 1:3–4;
Rev. 3:20

1. What have we been called into?

2. What does fellowship involve?

Father, how glad I am that when I talk to You I am not listening for an echo of my own voice; I am listening for the voice of the divine shepherd. You know my voice and I know Yours. What reassurance this gives me. Thank You. Amen.

Christianity is Christ

FOR READING & MEDITATION – ACTS 4:1–22

'there is no other name under heaven given to mankind by which we must be saved.' (v12)

Two days ago we mentioned that a group of theological lecturers claimed we should make more of the principles of Christ than of His person. 'Jesus is a controversial figure', they argued, 'so we must play down the person and play up His principles.' How different from the words of Archbishop William Temple – one of the foremost Christian leaders in Britain during the first half of the twentieth century – when he wrote: 'The supreme revelation is given in the life and person of Jesus. The revelation is not His teaching or His acts but Himself.

FURTHER STUDY

Acts 17:22–34; 1 Cor. 3:10–15

1. What contrasts did Paul make?

2. Why must we be careful?

Christianity is not a dedication to a system of rules or of thought, but a dedication to a person. This is unique among the religions of the world.'

In our multi-faith post-Christian society, which is largely informed by populist thoughts, it's important to continually raise the issue, and present it in every way we can, that the person of Jesus is central to the Christian faith. Christianity has its doctrines, but it is more than a doctrine; it has its creeds, but it is more than a creed; it has its traditions and sacraments, but it is more than rites or ceremonies; it has its institutions, but it is more than an institution. Christianity is Christ. Christian people are people who believe in God, and believe also that the way to God – the only way to God – is through Christ.

When we come in contact with the person – Jesus – then the principles embodied in the person take on strength and vitality. We want to practise the principles because He practised and embodied them. Principles become life as they are embodied in a person, otherwise they remain distant and the human heart is indifferent to them.

Gracious Father, You have shown us in Your Son that You practise what You long for us. 'For by all that God requires of me, I know that He Himself must be.' Let all Your principles become personal in me this day. Amen.

Next Issue

JAN/FEB 2021

Secure and Sure-footed

'He makes my feet like the feet of the deer', says the writer of Psalm 18:33, 'he causes me to stand on the heights.' 2020 seems to have been an extraordinary year, quite unlike any other. But even in times of extreme uncertainty, when we bring our deepest longings, fears and disappointments to God, we can stand firm even on shaky ground.

Join us next issue as we commence the New Year with a renewed hope in God, reminding ourselves that we can navigate any terrain when we allow Him to co-ordinate our heads, hearts and feet.

Every Day
with Jesus

JAN/FEB 2021

Secure and
Sure-Footed

'He makes my feet
like the feet of a deer;
he causes me to
stand on the heights.'
Psalm 18:33

Living life with Jesus. Every day   **CWR**

Also available as an
eBook/eSubscription

....

Please note: from the next issue, the price of your copy will be £3.49. For updated subscription prices, please see the order form at the back of these notes.

Obtain your copy from CWR, a Christian bookshop or your National Distributor.

The face of God

FOR READING & MEDITATION – 1 PETER 1:1–12

'*Though you have not seen him, you love him*' *(v8)*

'Jesus Christ,' said a small boy, 'puts a face on God.' How meaningful those words become at this Christmas season. Jesus is God's face. We are people who long for the personal. These words of Robert Browning are some that I love:

'Tis the weakness in strength that I cry for!
My flesh, that I seek in the Godhead,
I seek it and find it!
O Saul, it shall be a Face like my face
that receives Thee; a Man like to me,
Thou shalt love and be loved by, for ever.
A Hand like this hand shall throw open the gates
of new life to Thee.
See the Christ stand!

**FURTHER
STUDY**

John 20:24–29;
1 Tim. 2:5–6

1. What did
Thomas realise?

2. What did
Paul explain?

What if there were no flesh in the Godhead – no face like my face there? Then the Godhead would be awesome but not recognisable. The truth that there is a human face on the throne of God touches my heart in a way that nothing else could. It means I can stand in the presence of God knowing that alongside me will stand One who has lived on earth and knows our human condition because He has been like me in every way – Jesus. Jesus has worn my flesh, measured its frailty and is swift to save.

Robert Browning again:

That one dear face, far from vanishing
rather grows, and becomes
my universe that feels and knows.

Father, the thought of a person on the throne of God evokes a response in me that perhaps nothing else could. Jesus is so like me, yet so unlike me. I wait with joy for the day when I shall look upon His face. Amen.

No fleeting vision

FOR READING & MEDITATION – LUKE 1:67–80

*'Praise be to the Lord... because he has come to his people
and redeemed them.' (v68)*

We remind ourselves that the verse which is the centrepiece of our Christmas meditation is John 1:14: 'The Word became flesh and made his dwelling among us. We have seen his glory, the glory of the one and only Son, who came from the Father, full of grace and truth.' Let us think now about the words 'and made his dwelling among us'.

The thought behind those words in the original Greek is of someone 'tabernacling' with us, or pitching His tent among us. The revelation of God in Jesus was not a momentary rift in the clouds, a fleeting vision of what God is like. Jesus didn't sit on a cloud and pass on commands, or pick us up with some kind of celestial tongs and take us to heaven to avoid dirtying His fingers with the messy business of human living. No, He 'made his dwelling among us' – in the middle of our poverty, our temptations, our problems and choices, our hopes and disappointments.

Jesus spent 33 years on this earth, from cradle to grave. It was not long by earthly standards, but life depends not on the hours you put in but what you put into the hours. He revealed the character of God in the everyday in the same sort of surroundings where your character and mine is developed. He met life as you and I meet it – except that He demonstrated total dependence on the Father all the time. We demonstrate total dependence only some of the time. He performed no miracle to get out of any difficulty, and used His resources, not for Himself, but to meet needs in others. He lived a normal life, worked as a carpenter, ate food, took exercise, and so on. He lived among us and showed us how to live – by living.

FURTHER STUDY

Matt. 4:2;
13:53–58;
26:37–38;
John 4:6

1. Why did Christ's neighbours not think Him special?

2. How did Christ share our human experience?

Lord Jesus, how glad I am that I walk with one who has all the wisdom, all the power, all the grace I need. Thank You for showing me Your life in the middle of life. Now I know what life can be like for I have seen it – in You. Amen.

A day for thanksgiving

FOR READING & MEDITATION – MATTHEW 1:18–25

'you are to give him the name Jesus, because he will save his people from their sins.' (v21)

On this, the day we set apart to celebrate in a special way the birth of Jesus, how good it is to know we are celebrating not the birth of a principle, but the birth of a divine person. 'You have an advantage,' said a university professor in China to a Christian visiting the country, 'in that all the ideas in Christianity are embodied in a person.' 'The impersonal laid no hold on my heart', said Tulsidas, the great poet of India. It never does, for the human heart is personal and wants a personal response.

FURTHER STUDY

Luke 2:1–20

1. What did the angels and shepherds have in common?

2. Where were the shepherds to find the Lord and Saviour?

I love repeating the story of the boy who stood looking at the picture of his absent father and then, turning to his mother, said wistfully, 'I wish father would step out of the picture and hold me in his arms.' That young boy expressed the kind of deep longings felt by the human heart as we stand looking at the picture frame of the universe. We who have gazed at the picture of God in nature are impressed, but not satisfied. We want our Father to step out of the picture and meet us as a person.

The good news is that the Father has stepped out of the picture. This is the meaning of Christmas. Jesus is Immanuel – God with us. We hold our breath as the person steps out of the picture. Who would dare dream that God would send us His own Son? But He did. Since Jesus is 'the radiance of God's glory and the exact representation of his being' (Heb. 1:3), we look at the character of Jesus and know what God's character is like.

The Christmas Word can, in a sense, become flesh in me. Today and every day I think of Jesus' incarnation and of God's love for us. The Christian spirit is the Christmas spirit – extended throughout the whole year.

Gracious Father, as You sent Your Son to speak to us, so may I spread the message of Christmas. And not just today but every day. In Christ's name I pray. Amen.

'I take a bite'

FOR READING & MEDITATION – HEBREWS 4:1–16

'tempted in every way, just as we are – yet he did not sin.' (v15)

We continue meditating on the words, 'The Word became flesh and made his dwelling among us' (John 1:14). Jesus really did live among us. He resisted the temptation to live in any way other than 'among'.

A church leader once said that Jesus, during the temptation in the wilderness (Matt. 4:1–11), illustrates most clearly what it means to be 'among'. The first temptation (he claimed) was to live apart from us by using resources not available to ordinary mortals. This He rejected – He would eat as we eat. The second temptation (to live above us) He rejected also. He would not throw Himself down from the pinnacle of the Temple and then be carried back by angels. That would be living above the rest of humanity. The third temptation was to live as we live, by taking the devil's suggestion to worship him, to adopt his methods, and gain the kingdoms of the world. He rejected this temptation because although He identified with us in every way, He did not commit sin.

An American soldier tells how during the Vietnam War he saw a little girl who was starving and at once offered her a bite of his sandwich. 'No,' she said, 'it might be poisoned.' The soldier took a bite and said, 'I take a bite, you take a bite.' She watched him bite off a bit of the sandwich, chew it and swallow it, then did the same. In a sense, this is what Jesus did with us. The Bible tells us that He tasted death for every one of us (Heb. 2:9). But it is also true, that He tasted life for every one of us. He asks us to do nothing that He has not done. He was tempted in every way as we are, yet without sin. He knows us from within.

FURTHER STUDY

Matt. 4:1–11;
Heb. 5:1–10

1. How did Christ overcome temptation?

2. Why was it necessary for Him to be tempted?

Lord Jesus, how glad I am that You know me not just from the outside, but from the inside also. You lived 'among' us. For that I am and shall always be grateful. Amen.

See His glory

FOR READING & MEDIATION – JOHN 17:1–5

'I have brought you glory on earth by finishing the work you gave me to do.' (v4)

The next words we read in John 1:14 are these: 'We have seen his glory, the glory of the one and only Son, who came from the Father'. When John said, 'We have seen his glory', what did he mean? What would that 'glory' be?

I once asked a youth group what they thought John had in mind here when he said, 'We have seen his glory'. One young man suggested, 'It was the glory of being able to answer all questions.' I said, 'So His glory was in His knowledge and wisdom?' 'Yes,' replied the young man. A young woman then volunteered this: 'I think His glory lay in the fact that He was able to perform miracles.' I said, 'So His glory was in what He did?' 'Yes,' she agreed. Another young man said, 'I think His glory was the way in which He was able to go to the cross and give Himself sacrificially for us.' I said, 'So His glory was in His death?' 'Yes,' he replied. Although these were excellent suggestions, and showed much insight and imagination, they did not adequately answer the question. The glory of the Son of God lay not so much in what He did or what He said but in who He was.

FURTHER STUDY

Luke 9:28–36;
2 Cor. 4:4–6

1. What did the disciples see?
2. Where do we discover the glory of God?

Listen to the words in John 1:14 once again: 'the glory of the one and only Son, who came from the Father'. Jesus' glory is rooted in His uniqueness as 'the one and only Son'. It was intrinsic – something that emanated from Him and permeated everything He did. He certainly demonstrated glory in His knowledge, and glory in His wisdom, and glory in His deeds, but the real glory lay in who He was – the glory of His being. Knowledge, wisdom, power and all the other qualities flowed from His being. Being the 'Son, who came from the Father' was everything.

Lord Jesus, I praise You not only for what You did and what You said but for who You are. You are the one and only Son. I look at You and know there could be no other like You. Thank You that You are always with us. Amen.

A sinner's favourite word

FOR READING & MEDITATION – TITUS 2:1–15

'For the grace of God has appeared that offers salvation to all people.' (v11)

We come now to the final words of the amazing verse which has been central to our thinking at this Christmastime: 'The Word became flesh and made his dwelling among us. We have seen his glory, the glory of the one and only Son, who came from the Father, full of grace and truth' (John 1:14). It is interesting that John puts grace before truth. The first element in the Christian faith is 'grace' – an act of outgoing, forgiving love. Theologians say we should not put one attribute of God before another because they are all of equal importance in the Godhead, but to me it seems significant that John puts grace first and truth second. The first characteristic of God is love, and grace is love reaching down to a lost humanity in Jesus Christ. It is the Word of love become flesh.

There are many definitions of grace. One of my favourites is based on the acrostic: God's Riches At Christ's Expense. Another one I particularly like is 'love in action'. The one I like best, however, is the one that defines grace simply as 'unmerited favour'. Grace is love favouring us when we are not favourable, loving us when we are not lovable, accepting us when we are not acceptable, redeeming us when, in human terms, and by all the rules of the book, we are not redeemable.

The principal of the college where I was trained for the ministry, John Wallace, used to say that although the favourite word of angels might be love, the favourite word of sinners is grace. Love reaches out on the same level, he explained, but grace is a word with a stoop in it. Grace always bends to pick us up. Grace is love applied, the Word of love become flesh.

FURTHER STUDY

Titus 3:3–7;
2 Thess. 2:16–17

1. How are love and grace linked?

2. What definition of grace do you like?

Father God, how grateful I am for Your grace. Thank You for favouring me when I was not favourable, and loving me when I was not lovable. In Jesus' name. Amen.

Love is first

FOR READING & MEDITATION – PHILIPPIANS 2:1–11

'And being found in appearance as a man, he humbled himself by becoming obedient to death' (v8)

Today we continue to consider that final phrase from John 1:14: 'full of grace and truth'. Suppose John had said, 'full of truth and grace', then the emphasis would have been upon 'truth' in God. Although, as we said yesterday, we must be careful about making too much of the order of the words, it is my view that John put 'grace' before 'truth' for a reason.

Many of the cults affirm 'God is truth', yet it is not a declaration that we often use in the Christian Church. Gandhi acknowledged that 'God is truth', as, indeed, did many of the ancient philosophers. Jesus told us, 'I am the way and the truth and the life' (John 14:6), please notice He put 'way' before 'truth'. While it is absolutely right to say that 'God is truth', that is not the first quality to recognise in the Godhead. The first characteristic of God is love.

FURTHER STUDY

John 1:15–18;
8:3–11;
Acts 15:5–12

1. Contrast Moses and Jesus.

2. What was Peter's point?

If Scripture had said 'God is truth', then people could regard Christianity as a philosophy. But the Christian faith is not first and foremost a thought, a philosophy, but an act – an act of love invading history to redeem lost men and women. Grace, as we said yesterday, is love in action. Truth does come into the picture, of course, but it comes after grace. Why should this be so? In my view it is because in order to understand truth we have to 'see' it, not just hear about it. If truth is not seen in action, it is not seen, for truth not in action is truth verbal and not vital. You are not truth and I am not truth unless we are truth in our relationships, in our actions. So we see 'truth' through 'grace'. Grace is truth in gracious action. We see the nature of truth through the act – the Word made flesh.

Lord Jesus, You not only said, 'I am the truth', but showed us through Your acts what truth is: not a dry proposition but something liveable, lovable and personable. I am in awe at the wonder of it. Thank You, dear Saviour. Amen.

Truth is second

FOR READING & MEDITATION – 1 CORINTHIANS 10:23–33

'whatever you do, do it all for the glory of God.' (v31)

When it comes to describing God as both truth and grace, we are saying that grace is mentioned first. But although 'grace' comes first, 'truth' has to come next. Grace should not be regarded as overemotional sentimentality; it works within the framework of integrity and truth.

A missionary to a remote tribe in south-east Asia once told how those who had become Christians taught him the real meaning of grace when they said, 'Christianity is the only faith where you can't wangle God to get benefits out of Him.' They were used to a religion where you attempted to cajole, bribe, manipulate, and wangle your god in the hope that he would do you favours. Not so with Jesus. If we come to Him honestly, following His lead, we can receive everything we need. When we come with manipulative motives and keeping our distance, we end up receiving nothing. There are some who, although they do not recognise what they are doing, approach Jesus from the angle of following Him so that He, in turn, will give them what they want. They are interested in discipleship not so much because following is the one and only response to a Saviour such as He, but in order to obtain something – a supply of some need or some answer to prayer.

FURTHER STUDY

Matt. 6:1–8;
Luke 18:9–14

1. What truth did Jesus tell?

2. Contrast the Pharisee and tax collector.

While we all want to live a life that's pleasing to God, it's not that we need to please Him in order that He might grant His favours on us. That is trying to wangle things out of God – something the new Christians from the remote tribe knew instinctively was not necessary. As we give ourselves to Him, follow Him, obey Him, the pleasing takes care of itself. It is a consequence, not a cause, of our relationship with Him.

Lord Jesus, You are both grace and truth. This means I do not need to bribe You or manipulate You. But I can come to You honestly, following Your ways, and be granted everything I need. And for this I am thankful beyond words. Amen.

Flawless character

FOR READING & MEDITATION – 2 CORINTHIANS 5:11–21

'God made him who had no sin to be sin for us' (v21)

We end this year with a final look at the phrase 'full of grace and truth' (John 1:14). Notice we are told that the Word was 'full of grace and truth'. This means there are no contradictions in Christ's character – grace and ungrace, truth and untruth. In Him there is grace and only grace; truth and only truth. He never taught a principle that He did not practise, and never made a moral statement that He did not demonstrate in His life.

An African pastor, when introducing me to his church in Kisumu, East Africa said, 'Selwyn, come and tell us more about Jesus; we love to hear about a man who practised everything He preached.' When John told us that Jesus is full of grace and truth he was saying that in Him is a perfect unified person.

FURTHER STUDY

Luke 23:13–15, 41,47;
Heb. 7:11–28

1. What did people acknowledge about Christ?

2. What divided Jesus from other religious leaders?

Over the years I have met some wonderful Christians, but the more I have got to know and relate to them, the clearer their imperfections have become. No doubt the same could be said by others about me. What is my point? That Christians have flawed characters; some are more flawed than others. We have grace and we have ungrace; we have truth and we have untruth – albeit unconsciously.

Some have reached the stage in their spiritual development where there is far more grace than ungrace, and far more truth than untruth. They exhibit such fine qualities of character that they can be described as nearly perfect. Jesus, however, was not nearly perfect, He was absolutely perfect. 'Can any of you prove me guilty of sin?' He once asked a group of people (John 8:46). No one could find a flaw in Him. He is not only the best humanity has ever seen, but the best it will ever see. He is full of grace and truth.

Father, I too love to listen to a man who practised everything He preached. Let the beauty of Jesus' character be seen also in me – now and evermore. For the honour and glory of Your name I ask it. Amen.

Order form

4 Easy Ways To Order

1. Phone in your credit card order: **01252 784700** (Mon–Fri, 9.30am – 4.30pm)
2. Visit our online store at **cwr.org.uk/store**
3. Send this form together with your payment to: **CWR, Waverley Abbey House, Waverley Lane, Farnham, Surrey GU9 8EP**
4. Visit a Christian bookshop

For a list of our National Distributors, who supply countries outside the UK, visit cwr.org.uk/distributors

Your Details (required for orders and donations)

Full Name:

CWR ID No. (if known):

Home Address:

Postcode:

Telephone No. (for queries):

Email:

Publications

TITLE	QTY	PRICE	TOTAL
		Total Publications	

UK P&P: up to £24.99 = **£2.99**; £25.00 and over = **FREE**

Elsewhere P&P: up to £10 = **£4.95**; £10.01 – £50 = **£6.95**; £50.01 – £99.99 = **£10**; £100 and over = **£30**

Total Publications and P&P (please allow 14 days for delivery) **A**

Subscriptions* (non direct debit)

	QTY	PRICE (including P&P)			TOTAL
		UK	Europe	Elsewhere	
Every Day with Jesus (1yr, 6 issues)		£17.95	£22.50	Please contact nearest National Distributor or CWR direct	
Large Print *Every Day with Jesus* (1yr, 6 issues)		£17.95	£22.50		
Inspiring Women Every Day (1yr, 6 issues)		£17.95	£22.50		
Life Every Day (Jeff Lucas) (1yr, 6 issues)		£17.95	£22.50		
YP's: 11–14s (1yr, 6 issues)		£17.95	£22.50		
Topz: 7–11s (1yr, 6 issues)		£17.95	£22.50		
Total Subscriptions (subscription prices already include postage and packing)				**B**	

*Only use this section for subscriptions paid for by credit/debit card or cheque. For Direct Debit subscriptions see overleaf.

All CWR adult Bible reading notes are also available in **eBook** and **email subscription** format. Visit cwr.org.uk for further information.

Please circle which issue you would like your subscription to commence from:

JAN/FEB MAR/APR MAY/JUN JUL/AUG SEP/OCT NOV/DEC

How would you like to hear from us?

We would love to keep you up to date on all aspects of the CWR ministry, including; new publications, events & courses as well as how you can support us.

If you **DO** want to hear from us on email, please tick here [ ]

If you **DO NOT** want us to contact you by post, please tick here [ ]

Continued overleaf >>

You can update your preferences at any time by contacting our customer services team on 01252 784 700. You can view our privacy policy online at cwr.org.uk

<< See previous page for start of order form

Payment Details

☐ I enclose a cheque made payable to CWR for the amount of: **£** _____

☐ Please charge my credit/debit card.

Cardholder's Name (in BLOCK CAPITALS) _____

Card No. ☐☐☐☐ ☐☐☐☐ ☐☐☐☐ ☐☐☐☐

Expires End ☐☐ ☐☐ Security Code ☐☐☐

Gift to CWR ☐ Please send me an acknowledgement of my gift **C** ☐_____

Gift Aid (your home address required, see overleaf)

giftaid it I am a UK taxpayer and want CWR to reclaim the tax on all my donations for the four years prior to this ye and on all donations I make from the date of this Gift Aid declaration until further notice.*

Taxpayer's Full Name (in BLOCK CAPITALS) _____

Signature _____ **Date** _____

*I am a UK taxpayer and understand that if I pay less Income Tax and/or Capital Gains Tax than the amount of Gift Aid claimed on all my donations in that t year it is my responsibility to pay any difference.

GRAND TOTAL (Total of A, B & C) ☐_____

Subscriptions by Direct Debit (UK bank account holders only)

One-year subscriptions cost £17.95 and include UK delivery. Please tick relevant boxes and fill in the form below.

☐ *Every Day with Jesus* (1yr, 6 issues)
☐ Large Print *Every Day with Jesus* (1yr, 6 issues)
☐ *Inspiring Women Every Day* (1yr, 6 issues)
☐ *Life Every Day* (Jeff Lucas) (1yr, 6 issues)

☐ *YP's*: 11–14s (1yr, 6 issues)
☐ *Topz*: 7–11s (1yr, 6 issues)

Issue to commence from
☐ Jan/Feb ☐ Jul/Aug
☐ Mar/Apr ☐ Sep/Oct
☐ May/Jun ☐ Nov/Dec

CWR Instruction to your Bank or Building Society to pay by Direct Debit

Please fill in the form and send to: CWR, Waverley Abbey House, Waverley Lane, Farnham, Surrey GU9 8EP **Name and full postal address of your Bank or Building Society**

DIRECT Debi

To: The Manager Bank/Building Society

Address _____

_____

Postcode _____

Name(s) of Account Holder(s)

_____

Branch Sort Code
☐☐ ☐☐ ☐☐

Bank/Building Society Account Number
☐☐☐☐☐☐☐☐

Originator's Identification Number

4	2	0	4	8	7

Reference

☐☐☐☐☐☐☐☐☐☐☐☐☐☐☐☐☐☐

Instruction to your Bank or Building Society

Please pay CWR Direct Debits from the account detailed in this Instru subject to the safeguards assured by the Direct Debit Guarantee. I understand that this Instruction may remain with CWR and, if so, deta will be passed electronically to my Bank/Building Society.

Signature(s)

_____

Date _____

Banks and Building Societies may not accept Direct Debit Instructions for some types of account